Playing the Tuba at Midnight

The Joys & Challenges of Singleness

ROBERTA RAND

InterVarsity Press
Downers Grove, Illinois

InterVarsity Press® is the book-publishing division of InterVarsity Christian Fellowship®, a student movement active on campus at hundreds of universities, colleges and schools of nursing in the United States of America, and a member movement of the International Fellowship of Evangelical Students. For information about local and regional activities, write Public Relations Dept., InterVarsity Christian Fellowship, 6400 Schroeder Rd., P.O. Box 7895, Madison, WI 53707-7895.

All Scripture quotations, unless otherwise indicated, are taken from the HOLY BIBLE, NEW INTERNATIONAL VERSION®. NIV®. Copyright ©1973, 1978, 1984 by International Bible Society. Used by permission of Zondervan Publishing House. All rights reserved.

Cover illustration: Tim Nyberg

ISBN 0-8308-1690-9

Printed in the United States of America ♾

Library of Congress Cataloging-in-Publication Data has been requested.

19	18	17	16	15	14	13	12	11	10	9	8	7	6	5	4	3	2	1
10	09	08	07	06	05	04	03	02	01	00	99	98	97	96	95			

To Iris

*world traveler, bookworm,
tender spirit—and friend*

Acknowledgments

Thanks to:

Kurt Bruner for giving me the initial kick in the pants to write this book before someone else beat me to it.

Delores Perdue for her generous gift of a computer to facilitate future projects.

Bill Bell, Computer Wizard Extraordinaire, for patiently guiding me through the bewildering world of DOS and diskettes.

My counselor, Christie Lee, for her gentle insights.

My editor, Linda Doll, for many helpful suggestions and contributions.

My old friend Alan Adams, one of my "wise cheerleaders."

My wonderful, quirky, richly dysfunctional family for suggestions and contributions.

My dearest sister in spirit, Chris Engelhardt, who continues to inspire and amaze me with her gifts of speech, wit and discernment.

Finally, to all my strong, beautiful, single woman friends: This book's for you!

Preface

In 1992 I auditioned to appear as a contestant on Bill Cosby's revival of the old game show *You Bet Your Life*. During the audition process, I regaled the show's talent scouts with accounts of my colorful work history, teasing them with vague references to my career as an army counterintelligence agent ("I could tell you what I did, but then I'd have to kill you"). They all laughed.

Finally, I mentioned my ambition to write a book about the everyday struggles of living single. This seemed to intrigue one of my interviewers, who, I noted, was in her thirties and wore no wedding ring. When she continued to quiz me on the subject, I knew I was a shoo-in for game-show immortality.

Months later, as my game partner and I sweated under the glare of the studio lights, Mr. Cosby began his interrogation.

"Roberta Rand."

"Yessir."

"It says here you're single."

"That's right."

"Divorced?"

"Nope. Never married."

At that moment, sirens went off and down from the ceiling dropped a stuffed bird on a spring. Cosby pulled a cardboard sign out of the bird's beak. I had said the Secret Word—*married*. I won some cash, but I never did get to talk about my book.

The irony of that moment was not lost on this single soul, for it seems that *married* truly is, if not the secret word, then the word that holds the key to what our culture deems natural and necessary to a fulfilled, well-rounded life. Marriage is the institution that announces to the world we are finally all grown up. It provides proof that we are indeed desirable. It gives us permission to purchase matching china. It's sanctioned sex. It means never again having to face ruthless car salesmen alone.

Though we enlightened women of the nineties make a lot of noise about not needing a man to make us complete, somewhere in the recesses of memory our mothers' voices still haunt us with the promise that someday our handsome prince will come along. We remember all the years of planning the perfect wedding—should the bridesmaids wear taffeta or satin? Should we go with Paul Stookey's "Wedding Song" or the Carpenters' "We've Only Just Begun"?

As we nudge past age thirty, the wedding fantasies become a little frayed around the edges. For many of us, wide-eyed hopes for romance take on the grimly singleminded focus of the Terminator searching relentlessly for his target. At singles social events, we scan our sector for the few available men, then claw our way past a dozen other women with exactly the same goal in mind. Some of us become resigned to being single—yet secretly resent the hand God has dealt us. Others lose themselves in romance novels and wait passively for their luck to change. Sound familiar?

The reflections in this book offer candid insights on how to find peace of mind when your marriage dreams don't come true. They explore nitty-gritty issues like loneliness and altered friendships. They also take a humorous look at our sometimes quirky relationships with credit cards, chocolate and microwave dinners. One thing this book won't do is offer up pat solutions for all the unique frustrations of single living There are some aspects of this journey for which platitudes are roughly as effective as icing on a cement birthday cake—pretty to look at, but the hard stuff is still underneath. Maybe we would like someone to simply acknowledge that singleness in a pairs-dominated culture is just hard sometimes. But it also has its special joys. We'll take a look at that too.

Playing the Tuba at Midnight is for and about the woman who perhaps hasn't reconciled all the conflicting feelings she has about her singleness, yet desires to live fully in the imperfect present—regardless of her marital status. Maybe the ideas presented here will be just one more tool to help you navigate the sometimes turbulent skies of a couples' world. It can be a bumpy journey, but it is not one without hope.

1
When Your Best Friend Gets Married

The year was 1983. The place was Germany. Through sheer coincidence—and in accordance with the needs of the U.S. Army—my best friend, Chris, and I were stationed together in the lovely two-thousand-year-old city of Augsburg. Uncannily, our personal lives, our careers, even our thought patterns up to that time had always run on a parallel course. Now here we were, two women pushing thirty, reluctantly single, but making the most of this adventure in Europe.

One spring evening as we strolled Augsburg's cobblestone streets, I shared with Chris something I had heard on the radio. A famous actress was being interviewed. She said her life didn't really begin until she got married.

Somehow we concluded that, coming from a celebrity, this

must be a profound truth. The twinkling lights of downtown Augsburg seemed to dim a little as we both reflected on our pathetic status as "old maids."

Oh well. At least we had each other.

Fast forward to December 1989—Chris's wedding day. It was an elaborate ceremony. Afterward, as the happy couple ducked through a gauntlet of crossed swords, I snapped pictures and smiled through my tears. I prayed that she would look my way as she exited the church, but she swept by and was gone. My last close single friend had finally left the starting gate of life—and left me feeling abandoned, desolate and angry. I grieved for this loss, for I knew our friendship would never be the same. There would be no more long phone conversations between Missouri and Colorado. From now on, her friends would be "couple" friends. If I came to visit, we would be a threesome—Chris's husband, Dana, my friend by default. When she had a baby, the little contact we had would dwindle even further.

Chris became like the phantom limb that "itches" long after it has been amputated. I wasn't prepared for the change in our decade-long friendship and the void her departure left in my life. I resented her husband for taking her away and I resented God for not giving me a husband too.

As the months turned into a year, then two years, I slowly adjusted to the reality that things were never going back to the way they used to be. Although I didn't recognize them at the time, the stages of grief were slowly wending their way through my psyche. I turned my attention to other things. Talents and hobbies which along the way had been misplaced once more piqued my interest. I joined a writer's group and took a class in metalsmithing. As I became immersed in writing and art projects, first days, then weeks went by in which Chris barely crossed my mind. A subtle transformation was taking place as my identity and self-esteem hinged less on the "strokes" from others and more on creative self-expression.

One day it occurred to me that my life did not have to follow the path that Chris's life—or anyone else's life—had taken. I began to experience exhilaration in the fresh insight that God had a plan for my life which was totally unique—whether or not it included marriage.

Coincidentally, Chris and I started to communicate again. I traveled to Missouri for a visit last spring. I was able to share her joy in her baby son, and I had some good conversations with Dana. We spent a brief but happy time together musing about the turns our lives had taken. About once a month we talk on the phone. Our chats are not the marathon gabfests they once were, but the conversations are meaningful and no longer marked by neediness and resentment.

I have learned from this experience that deep friendships need not be destroyed by the ebb and flow of time. Yes, our lives may take separate courses. Things may not stay the same. But perhaps that's how it should be. When we finally learn to release our hold on things we are not meant to control, we become free to live in the present and experience growth—in our friendships, in ourselves and in our understanding of God's will for our lives.

Thinking back to our conversation so many years ago on that street in Augsburg, I realize we were wrong to conclude that life starts when you get married. Life starts at this moment, regardless of the presence of a wedding ring.

There is a time for everything,
and a season for every activity under heaven. (Eccles 3:1)

2

Soap Scum, Cookie Dough and Buffing Machines

A couple of years back, a short-lived TV comedy series called *The Days and Nights of Molly Dodd* featured a scene in which a single, thirtysomething Molly sits at a piano, plunking out a tune with one hand, holding a bowl of cereal with the other and occasionally petting her cat while both the TV and the radio blare in the background. I remember laughing out loud as I recognized myself in that scene. Absurd moments occur in the solitude of a single person's home.

With responsibility for no one but ourselves, we are pretty much free to do everything at once or nothing at all at any hour of the day or night. We can eat our microwave dinners while sprawled on the couch watching *Jeopardy,* then dispose of the cardboard box and plastic spoon—voilà! no mess!—in time to make it to our latest codependency workshop. We can practice the tuba at midnight. We don't have to make the bed or scrub the bathtub (it may be soap scum, but it's *our* soap scum). We can drink directly from the milk carton or spoon raw cookie dough into our mouths with impunity—although implanted in all our brains at birth is a computer chip programmed with our mother's voice warning us of the horrific consequences of such poor habits. You know that voice—it reminds you that insect larvae in raw cookie dough will, when swallowed, metamorphose into something akin to the thing that popped out of the guy's chest in the movie *Alien*.

Yes, when it comes to lifestyle choices—from personal hygiene to meal schedules—singles have a plethora of options about which most married people can only wax nostalgic. If there is a "down" side to all this unfettered freedom, it is this: For those of us who struggle with self-esteem problems and borderline addictions, occasional sloppy behavior can easily degenerate into depravity and excess.

> Like a city whose walls are broken down
> is a man who lacks self-control. (Prov 25:28)

The prospect of a lonely weekend triggers a frantic visit to the local Safeway. We stock up on Oreos and proceed to eat our way through the weekend. After an angry run-in with a supervisor, we career over to the mall and charge hundreds of dollars in Liz Claiborne separates. Rejection by a love interest sends us into an emotional tailspin. We may end up in places, activities or relationships that offer temporary and very false comfort. It's not a pretty sight, but we rationalize, *Who has to know?* The prophet Jeremiah put it this way:

> "Although you wash yourself with soda

18

and use an abundance of soap,
> the stain of your guilt is still before me,"
> > declares the Sovereign LORD. (Jer 2:22)

Who has to know? Only you and the One who counts most.

Back in my Army days, we had these monstrous industrial-strength buffing machines. The one in our barracks weighed probably two hundred pounds and consisted of a large rotating buffer with a motor attached. The drive-train protruded from the machine and had two handles at the top with an accelerator and a brake, making it operate much like a motorcycle . . . theoretically. The problem was, if one didn't get a death grip on the handle and brace it firmly against the body with elbows locked, the machine veered wildly out of control, swerving into any poor soldier who happened to be in the wrong place at the wrong time. It took me a while to master the beast, but when I did, what a good feeling it was! The results were barracks floors so polished that I could see my own reflection.

Bad habits unchecked can become like the out-of-control buffing machine. You don't have to make your bed in the morning or clean the mildew from the shower floor. VROOOOOOOM!BAM@#*! Legions of cockroaches may party hearty on the free-form sculpture of dirty dishes balanced precariously in the kitchen sink. ZWISH!THWUMP@#*! You may even survive for a while on a diet of Ding-Dongs and Slim Jims. ERRRRRRR!CRASH@#*! But taken to an extreme, such a lifestyle eventually takes its toll on your health and your self-esteem.

Bringing order and discipline into your life may be akin to wrestling that bucking, thrashing buffing machine into submission. Yet when you start to realize order in the small details of your life, you may begin to tame your inner demons as well. Sweep those cobwebs out of the corners of the living room, and you may feel the cobwebs in your brain also begin to clear. Chase the dust bunnies from under the bed—the solution to a personal problem may suddenly present itself. Little by little, dish by dirty dish, Hefty bag by Hefty bag, you will feel your outlook start to brighten—just like the sparkling porcelain surface of your newly emptied kitchen sink.

If you are like me, when you finally arrive at a place where you must create order out of the chaos of your physical surroundings—or else melt down like a nuclear power plant on *tilt*—you may feel immobilized by the sheer enormity of the task. Where do you start?

You start with the simplest, least brain-straining thing. Clutter, perhaps. How about throwing away that Publishers Clearinghouse envelope? You *know* your chances of winning are one in a hundred gazillion. Ain't no Prize Patrol gonna come to your house. Besides, that envelope is two years old! Toss it, followed by the little pile of foil wrappers from the bag of Hershey's kisses you polished off last night. Don't be distracted by the mounds of dirty clothes, old newspapers and dusty windowsills that you've yet to address. Concentrate on the little things in one room; perhaps break the task down even further, to one corner of a room. You will find that as you methodically accomplish one small task at a time, a pattern will emerge and the process will take on a life of its own.

Not all of life's problems are solved by a clean house. Sometimes a chaotic, disorganized environment is a symptom of a deeper emotional problem. There is also the reverse problem of obsessive-compulsive behavior in which you can never get your house clean and organized enough. But these situations are not what I'm writing about. All of us have areas of excess in our lives which defy taming. Perhaps it's an unhealthy dependence on men to meet our emotional needs. Or a volatile temper. Maybe it's a tendency to soothe unpleasant emotions with food. In these times when twelve-step groups exist for every conceivable addiction/compulsion, we needn't feel that there is nowhere to get help.

But we should also recognize that on this side of heaven we will never get ourselves completely "fixed." For those of us who exist somewhere in the middle on the continuum of good mental health, just knowing a few practical tips for getting unstuck can save us big counseling bills and help us know that we really do have the inner resources to take control of the out-of-control buffing machines in our lives.

And like Mom said. Always wear clean underwear. You never know when you might get hit by a bus.

For the grace of God that brings salvation has appeared to all men. It teaches us to say "No" to ungodliness and worldly passions, and to live self-controlled, upright and godly lives in this present age, while we wait for the blessed hope—the glorious appearing of our great God and Savior, Jesus Christ, who gave himself for us to redeem us from all wickedness and to purify for himself a people that are his very own, eager to do what is good. (Tit 2:11-14)

3

The Sounds of Silence

Escape. My house teems with evidence of attempts to escape from periodic attacks of panic, loneliness and boredom. Cassette tapes of waves lapping at an anonymous beach were supposed to ease me through a dreary, vacationless winter. Blank canvases and pristine tubes of oil paint mark an early impulse to shake off the old me and adopt the identity of Fascinating Woman of Artistic Vision. Cupboards bulging with cans of SlimFast and leftover Nutri-System salad dressings testify to abandoned plans to drop weight. Having failed the diet endeavor, bottles of L'Oreal await my next attempt to effect an inner transformation through the simple application of hair color.

When I'm unhappy at my job, bored in my personal life or

disgusted with the woman in the mirror, it's easy to opt for the quick fix or the impulsive gesture. Rather than confront an unpleasant situation at work, I'll scan the want ads and update my résumé. Instead of nursing a damaged friendship, I'll bury my nose in *People* magazine. Rather than wrestle with my relationship with God, I'll go shopping. I'm so easily distracted. And the culture I live in is more than happy to accommodate my compulsion to avoid introspection.

At times, the idea of being alone with my thoughts is about as attractive as treading water in a tank full of hungry sharks. Though I frequently travel alone, I am never without a book, a Walkman, a notebook—*something* to keep me distracted. Do I really want to hear God's voice? Sure—as long as the stereo is on and there are a few friends around for company. God may very well speak in the midst of such circumstances, but am I listening?

I read recently about a monastery in the mountains above Aspen, Colorado. Individuals seeking spiritual renewal make the trek to this remote hideaway and stay for a week or more in spartan huts, sans television or radio. Seeking to supplant the noise of the world with a silence that harkens only for the voice of God, they immerse themselves in the Word and wait on heavenly insight. It sounds so divinely ascetic. The mountains. The wind in the trees. All that . . . *nature*. Unfortunately, something in my jittery psyche is ill at ease with the idea of an expanse of unstructured time devoid of the pacifying hum of "civilization." The agitated synapses in my brain yearn to create a plan, color in the blank page, hang a picture on the empty wall. Like an overzealous bricklayer, I rush in with my trowel full of verbiage to fill in awkward gaps in conversations. *God, I want to listen, but I can't stand the silence!*

24

I don't know if a forced time alone in a mountain retreat with a bunch of monks is what it takes to get us "noise junkies" in touch with God's voice. It might do to ask ourselves what it is about silence that scares us so much.

Perhaps it's the intrusive voice of a critical parent. Or an image of a personal failure for which we can't seem to forgive ourselves. Maybe it's the specter of a loss which we have yet to mourn. We sense those images, those voices rumbling ominously in the distance, just beyond our wall of noise. And it takes every ounce of emotional energy to hold them there. Sadly, until we allow the natural process of grief to invade our emotional wounds, neither will we experience the soothing ministrations of the Great Physician. His voice will remain garbled and indistinct—muffled beneath all those layers of noise.

A strange thing happened to the prophet Elijah one day:

The LORD said, "Go out and stand on the mountain in the presence of the LORD, for the LORD is about to pass by."

Then a great and powerful wind tore the mountains apart and shattered the rocks before the LORD, but the LORD was not in the wind. After the wind there was an earthquake, but the LORD was not in the earthquake. After the earthquake came a fire, but the LORD was not in the fire. And after the fire came a gentle whisper. When Elijah heard it, he pulled his cloak over his face and went out and stood at the mouth of the cave.

Then a voice said to him, "What are you doing here, Elijah?" (1 Kings 19:11-13)

It may take strong medicine to wean you and me from the noisemakers in our lives. But when it finally happens, I suspect we will hear the same gentle voice Elijah heard on that day after the wind had passed and the earth had settled. And what might we expect him to say? Perhaps he will tell us to forget about changing our hair and taking up all those exotic hobbies we really care nothing about. He might urge us to stop "looking for love in all the wrong places." Unplug the TV and the stereo. Stop running away from the silence. Because in the silence rests our hope. In the silence, a friend is waiting.

Be still, and know that I am God. (Ps 46:10)

4
Tick . . . Tick . . . Tick

A hit song from a few years ago told the story of a single woman in her thirties who sees babies everywhere and longs for a child of her own—but knows that her time is running out. The song seemed to strike a chord with a lot of women—many of them on the eighties career fast track—who saw a parallel to their own lives in those bittersweet lyrics. These women were experiencing their first pangs of panic over the shrinking biological possibility that they would experience motherhood. In their twenties and early thirties, they had calculated a comfortable cushion of years left in which to marry and begin a family. But now the shrinking pool of marriageable men was looking more like a shallow puddle. And for the first time they were forced to admit that there are some body processes which Jazzercise and alfalfa sprouts simply won't postpone.

There may be no sound that resonates as loudly in a single woman's psyche as her biological clock winding down to profound and irreversible silence. At thirty-nine, I realize my own days for conceiving and bearing children are numbered. Even allowing for another couple of years in which to meet and marry the Man of My Dreams, odds are shrinking that I'll have the opportunity to pass on my own unique set of genes and neuroses to another generation. Like a million other single baby-boomer women, I am coming to terms with what the Bible so affirmingly calls "barrenness."

Menopause. It's one of those words we heard rarely when we were growing up—and if we did, it was spoken in a stage whisper. The preferred, more delicate and somewhat mysterious phrase was "change of life": "Aunt Earlene is going through *the change of life.*" As if there were only one in a life. When I was younger, I pictured menopausal women as somewhere between Auntie Em in *The Wizard of Oz*—all sagging breasts and faded housedresses—and a sixtyish Joan Crawford with a crazed look in her eye and inch-long fingernails poised to strike. Bitter women with dried-up wombs and dried-up lives. *Yeccch.*

But wait a minute. I don't resemble Auntie Em. Or Joan Crawford. Neither do most of the women I know. As we thirtysomethings age, we have to search out a new, improved attitude toward menopause along with the real and symbolic losses this passage represents. Our whole lives we have pursued with varying degrees of fervor those elusive dreams of matrimony and motherhood—images that speak of a longing to nest and nurture. Menopause doesn't just put a dent in those dreams, it clubs them repeatedly. It is a transition that forces a shift in our thinking about what defines us as women. Who are we, if not wives and mothers?

It is all too easy to fall into the trap of viewing the end of our childbearing years as the death of our womanly worth. But we need to resist stereotypical thinking about age and where we should be at certain times in our lives.

Which brings me to the subject of prisms. I love prisms. I have all shapes and sizes hanging in the windows around my house. As the sun makes its arc from east to west, the faceted pieces of crystal separate the rays so they shimmer in variegated patterns across the walls of my living room. Sometimes I sit for long minutes in silence, mesmerized by the shifting choreography of light and shadow. Some pools of color quiver and ripple like water. Others move like bright starbursts on a ballroom floor.

Whenever I become fixated on a desire—be it marriage or babies—it serves me well to recall lessons learned from prisms. The Bible compares God to light. How does that light shine on and through me? If God is light, then it is reasonable to view myself as a prism through which he directs that light to be refracted into the myriad facets of his aspect and his will. That will can be manifested in infinite ways—and like the refracted light cast by a prism, it is mysterious and breathtaking in its uniqueness.

Looking out the window at the flat, diffused light of a winter day, a woman might conclude that this must be the only definition of light. She looks around at all her friends and coworkers who are married with children and naturally assumes that marriage + babies = happiness. What else could there be? And she hangs on obstinately to her definition of happiness, unwilling or afraid to consider a different equation.

Purchase a prism and hang it in a sunny window. Take time to contemplate the play of light on the walls. Unclench the fist that has held so fast to this one dream. Expose it to the light. It may be hard to concede that God could have bigger and better plans for you than any you could have dreamed for yourself—but believe it. And begin now by throwing back the shutters and inviting him to shine his divine light through you.

"For I know the plans I have for you," declares the LORD, *"plans to prosper you and not to harm you, plans to give you hope and a future." (Jer 29:11)*

5

Thinkin' Old

In 1994 I sat glued to my TV set along with the rest of the planet's population, watching the unfolding drama of the winter Olympics. Aside from the Tonya Harding-Nancy Kerrigan soap opera, I was fascinated with the men's figure-skating competition. I had followed Brian Boitano's skating career from his triumphant performance in the 1988 Olympics to a professional career that shut him out of the Olympics in 1992 and now to the electric moment of his long-awaited comeback. It had the potential to be one of those "joy of victory" moments shown repeatedly for posterity on *Wide World of Sports*.

A hush fell over the arena as Brian, in black tights and silk poet's shirt, skated to center ice. The graceful arms came up like angel wings. A few preliminary jumps and spins. Then he picked up speed, reversed his body on the ice and looked over his shoulder. A collective sucking in of breath and time stopped.

When he fell down on his first triple axel, I had to look away from the screen. Commentators mercilessly played the video-tape over and over again in slow motion, then followed it with a replay of Boitano's flawless gold-medal performance from 1988. One by one, a boyish Boitano ticked off triple axels, spins and double toe loops. As the videotape progressed, commentators pointed out the moves Brian had executed in 1988 that, due to age or injury, he was now unable to perform.

Wait a minute, I protested at the TV. The guy is just thirty years old! Calgary was only six years ago, for heaven's sake. And then I was possessed by a thought which both frightened and fascinated me with its morbid implications: From the day we are born, we are all dying by increments. Inch by inch. Varicose vein by varicose vein. It just shows up more dramati-cally in thoroughbred athletes who push their bodies to the limit.

Lately, I hear the phrase "I'm old" creeping into my speech. A friend of mine who just turned forty shared that she too is troubled by this insidious phrase cropping up in conversations with younger friends and coworkers. As if youth wasn't fleeting enough, she and I have shifted our minds into an "old mode." What's the matter with us? Whether out of a fear of the unknown, an addiction to routine or just plain laziness, we have begun to write off novelty and adventure as things to be experienced only by people under thirty. Well, I recognize the problem and I'm gonna fight it!

The phrase "I'm old" should be exorcised from our vocabularies at all costs. "I'm old" stunts the imagination and curtails motivation. It deceives us into thinking we have no time left.

Life is indeed short, and all too soon our bodies betray us. But we are foolish to accelerate the process by offering up an "I'm old" defense of what amounts to throwing away good years and vital brain matter in the slavish belief that we are defined by a number. No, you and I don't have to climb a mountain to prove we can still hang with the kids of Generation X. But we can expand our horizons.

Learn a language. Get involved in a political campaign. Take an Outward Bound adventure vacation. Let's not be afraid to pursue long-deferred dreams. To quote that famous sentiment expressed by poet Dylan Thomas, "Rage against the dying of the light."

One of my favorite movies is *Shirley Valentine*. Shirley is a middle-aged housewife, drained of her once bubbly joie de vivre by years of playing the dutiful wife and mother to ungrateful children and an insensitive husband. When she announces to her family and friends her intention of accepting a female buddy's offer of a trip to Greece, her scandalized family attempts to dissuade her at every turn. Middle-aged women don't do those things, they tell her.

At one point, in total discouragement, she scolds herself: "You're forty-two years old, Shirley. What are you thinking?"

She almost talks herself out of it until her own inner voice urges her on with the same words spoken in a new way: "Shirley, you are *only* forty-two years old!"

The years etched in her face literally fade away as she begins to explore who she is beyond the context of a dreary routine and a stale marriage. And what she learns ultimately reignites that youthful spark and breathes new life into her relationship with her husband.

Such experiences are available to you and me if we can just shake off "old" thinking. Most of the barriers we perceive to be blocking our goals are either self-imposed or ones the media and our culture have convinced us are real. And, in a way, imaginary barriers are the hardest to overcome. But monitor your thoughts and words. Are you thinking old? Talking old? If you are, take heed of the immortal words of Barney Fife and "Nip it! Nip it in the bud!" Then take the risk. You may be surprised to see those so-called insurmountable barriers come crashing down with no more than the nudge of a finger.

Praise the LORD, O my soul,
  and forget not all his benefits—
who forgives all your sins
  and heals all your diseases,
who redeems your life from the pit
  and crowns you with love and compassion,
who satisfies your desires with good things
  so that your youth is renewed like the eagle's. (Ps 103:2-5)

6

House of Cards

It looks so innocuous, that palm-sized rectangle of plastic with your name officially stamped on the front. But when you are lonely or bored or frustrated, it can take on almost mystical powers—transporting you, at least for a little while, to a place where troubles evaporate like the effervescent halo over a glass of Alka-Seltzer.

You can sense the excitement mounting as you cruise the mall parking lot—a spot opens up right in front of Penney's. It must be a sign from God, you rationalize, and you make your way breathlessly to the entrance. Once inside, the seductive smells of the perfume counter infiltrate your nasal passages like a mind-altering drug, banishing any notions of fiscal restraint. Feeling especially in need of a mood pick-me-up, you pick out the jumbo size of your favorite designer fragrance. "Cash or charge?" the saleswoman chirps. "Charge," you reply confidently, pulling out your card. The authoritative *wunk-chunk* of the imprint machine as it slides across carbon copies fills you with a comforting sense of power and the reassurance that your life isn't out of control after all. *Wunk-chunk.* Stress dissipates. *Wunk-chunk.* Worries disappear. *Wunk-chunk.* Euphoria sets in.

Incapacitated by credit card delirium, you are convinced that the new silk blouse, the CD, the glossy bag crammed with makeup "essentials" are all that's needed to deliver you from cellulite, job dissatisfaction and an empty love life. Slipping the little rectangle of plastic back into your wallet, you sigh contentedly. Life is beautiful. All is right with the world.

But credit-card highs eventually wear off, and, like Cinderella ignominiously skidding along on her behind in the company of a pumpkin and a few disoriented mice, you eventually wake up squinting into the glaring reality that expensive makeup and new clothes have not changed your life. The eye shadow did not make you lose forty pounds overnight, the silk blouse has not increased your popularity, and the CD featuring dolphin squeals has not raised your self-esteem. As you stare at the clothes unceremoniously crammed into your closet, then at the half-dozen lipsticks standing on your dresser in almost identical shades of peach, you puzzle, *What happened to the magic?* You thought for sure that the right lipstick would make you a happy person forever.

To top off your shopping hangover, the inevitable bill arrives and you can't even remember what you bought that justifies the stress of making minimum monthly payments while trying to ensure there's enough fuel in the tank to get you back and forth to work until your next paycheck. Never mind that you'll be eating Hamburger Helper minus the hamburger for the next week.

The insidious thing about credit cards is that the debt mounts so quickly, and the small payments are initially so painless, that we hardly notice ourselves being sucked into what amounts to indentured servitude. With our egos stroked by offers of "gold" cards and ever-increasing credit limits, we mindlessly go along with the credit-card company's schemes, never bothering to calculate the actual price we are paying for items that will wear out long before they're paid for. Most of us learn only from hard experience just how dangerous credit cards can be.

Married people and single people both struggle with the problem, but with more unstructured time, more disposable income and less accountability than our married counter-parts, we single women are especially vulnerable to spending addictions. Such distractions ensure that we can hold off just a little longer dealing with the sin in our lives.

I've been there myself. I lived comfortably for years on small incomes without credit cards. Then, in my early thirties, I began making a good salary that set me up for offers from numerous card companies. During that same time period, I was also living with extreme bouts of loneliness and a high-stress job I dreaded going to each day. Already nursing a lot of escape fantasies, I was easily lured by fawning pitches for "preapproved" cards.

It wasn't long before I was juggling several different monthly statements, paying only the minimum payment on each one. When a new offer came in the mail for a card with a lower interest rate, I would do my duty as a responsible consumer and shift all my balances to the new card. Of course, when that card got "maxed out," I resorted to consolidation loans. And I never thought I had a problem—until I lost my job and all my fiscal chickens came home to roost.

During the year I was unemployed, my impeccable credit rating nosedived. Token payments on astronomical balances were met with disdain by unsympathetic phone henchmen from VISA and MasterCard. When I finally found a new job and reestablished a regular income, I turned the whole mess over to Consumer Credit Counseling Service. One of the conditions of repaying my debts through them was that I destroy all my credit cards. It hasn't been easy. But what has been even harder are all the plans I had to put on hold while I methodically paid off $9,000 in old debts.

I will soon be debt-free. And God has used this time to teach me some hard lessons about self-discipline and deferred gratification. But I will never have those four years back. Doing time on a debt-management plan is exactly that: doing time. It means that big purchases like a home will remain on hold indefinitely. It means no fancy vacations. It may mean a retirement postponed by years. All because of the mistaken notion that the perfect lipstick will make you happy.

Nothing puts the kibosh on your dreams like deep debt. If you see yourself slipping into credit-card quicksand or if you are already mired in the muck, don't put off getting help. The sooner you get into a debt-management program and also deal with the underlying emotional triggers that make you spend, the sooner you can get on with your life. Once debt-free, you will no longer be wasting God's gift of time worrying about how you'll pay the bills. Instead, you can turn your focus to things that have eternal value—people, relationships and a life that glorifies God.

Do not work for food that spoils, but for food that endures to eternal life, which the Son of Man will give you. On him God the Father has placed his seal of approval. (Jn 6:27)

But he said to me, "My grace is sufficient for you, for my power is made perfect in weakness." Therefore I will boast all the more gladly about my weaknesses, so that Christ's power may rest on me. (2 Cor 12:9)

7

Plan B

There is a phenomenon familiar to long-distance runners. It is that point in a run when leg muscles pushed to their maximum seize up in excruciating cramps, lungs strain against the chest cavity like overinflated balloons and the body will simply no longer be subordinate to a bullying mind. They call it "hitting the wall."

Something like this occurred in the summer Olympic games in Los Angeles in 1984, when a female Swedish athlete running a marathon event began to wilt in the sweltering California sun. Passed by other runners, she fell farther and farther behind. When she staggered into the Olympic stadium for the remaining few laps of the race, she was alone on the track—disoriented and in obvious agony. One leg had given out, and she dragged it along behind her while weaving like a drunk back and forth across the lanes. Some thought she would drop dead before she crossed the finish line. Officials debated whether to call a halt to her dangerous quest. When medical personnel tried to escort her off the track, she waved them away.

As she doggedly pushed her tortured body toward the finish line, time took on the sluggish, compressed quality described by survivors of head-on car collisions ("Everything seemed to be happening in slow motion"). Finally, after an eternity of seconds, she crossed the finish line and crumpled to the ground. Her graceless, life-threatening ordeal was over. Never mind that she was within a hair of being an Olympic footnote—the first athlete to die in the marathon event while the world looked on in morbid fascination. She had finished the race. Any questions about the wisdom of her pursuit evaporated with the collective sigh of relief uttered by several million armchair athletes watching tensely from their recliners.

Hitting the wall doesn't pertain just to athletes. I've felt it; so have you: being stopped dead in your tracks by factors over which you have no control. Circumstances in which no amount of preparation or positive thinking will alter a negative outcome. Maybe the dream was a relationship that didn't work out. Or a promising career that never took off due to bad timing. It may have been an opportunity closed to you as a consequence of your own bad choices or moral lapses in the past. It could be any dream sidelined by illness or injury or loved ones whose needs have taken precedence over your own. We can all rest assured that, on this planet spinning on its tilted axis, "the best-laid plans of mice and men will surely go astray."

Whatever the event or villain that frustrates our plans, as

Christians we are encouraged that, in the great scheme of things, our failures are just well-placed stones in the cosmic stream of a master plan. Rather than frustrating God's purposes, they ensure the confluence of events to bring about his perfect will. The thing that trips us up as human beings is our inability to wrap our small brains around a very big picture.

Learning our limitations. Choosing our battles. Exchanging impossible dreams for possible ones. Staying in the race even when the rules have changed and someone has moved the finish line. That is what those of us frustrated with our singleness must learn to do. Things didn't work out the way we planned. So, what's plan B?

Years ago, I decided to hike to the top of a mountain, setting out confidently on the easy zigzag trail. About halfway up, the way turned rocky and steep. Another hundred yards and my knees turned to water. At the high altitude, my breath came in shallow gasps. I plunked down on a rock. The sun was dropping quickly in the sky, and I calculated that at the rate of my ascent, it would be dark long before I made it to the top. As I turned my glance away from the daunting, vertical cascade of rocks that loomed above me, back toward the way I had just come, I found myself gazing down upon a breathtaking sight. Out of a swirling mist of clouds leaped a perfect rainbow. It hung there for a minute or two, and then, as the afternoon sun dipped a little farther down in the sky, it disappeared.

There, in that brief interlude, resting among rocks drenched in golden sunlight, was the quiet assurance, *This is as good as it gets*. Halfway up the mountain, I had been rewarded with a mountaintop experience.

It is a good thing to have goals. And it is admirable to

accomplish a hard thing. But we need to remind ourselves that we are not made great by earthly achievements. Nor do we learn our most profound lessons in life through winning. For humility is more often a byproduct of failure than of triumph.

We can take comfort in the knowledge that there is nobility in effort—even effort interrupted. When the goals we have dedicated our lives to seem to elude our grasp like the brass ring on a merry-go-round, perhaps it would serve us well to pause in the pursuit and reassess. Is this thing I want so much really the thing that would be best for me? Have I exchanged a life rooted in the present for some romantic obsession that exists only in the climate-controlled hothouse of my own imagination? In my feverish quest for this goal, am I missing God's true calling for my life? These are hard questions to confront, especially when they may mean abandoning dreams that have come to define our whole identities. When we come to such a place, the healthy response is to pick up the pieces of our shattered dreams and mold them into something new. Using the wisdom that only failure can teach, we can begin to model our lives a little less on our own blueprints and a little more on God's.

The human mind may devise many plans,
but it is the purpose of the LORD that will
be established. (Prov 19:21 NRSV)

8
Looking Good

That woman. You know who I'm talking about. The one whose hair, nails, makeup and wardrobe are always perfectly coiffed, manicured and coordinated. She layers her fragrances. Her underwear always matches. Her home is immaculate, with sparkling kitchen, track lighting and mauve everything in the bathroom (toilet brushes are stored discreetly out of sight). Her late-model car is the same way—Armoralled inside and out and never used as a repository for overdue library books or bags of kitty litter.

I call her the Mauve Woman. She haunts my existence like an elusive goddess of Perfect Womanhood. But my attempts to duplicate her put-together persona are prone to go awry, as I invariably arrive at work with an unruly cowlick and petrified oatmeal adhered like a tacky corsage to the lapel of my new Chaus suit. And while the Mauve Woman's career runs right on track—she glides up the ladder of job success with nary a misstep—my own work life has been characterized by a series of false starts, periods of underemployment and unemployment, and a résumé that charts a lifelong search for identity and self-esteem. Likewise with the personal life. The Mauve Woman's love life is as tidy as her household, with no shameless attempts to win the wrong man's affections or embarrassing scenes when things didn't work out.

She really is a devil, this Mauve Woman. But if the truth be told, she is just one of a cast of imaginary women who daily tug me this way and that, leaving me confused about who I'm supposed to be. The Red Woman tells me to be bolder and more self-assertive. The Green Woman won't allow me to enjoy the good things in life because somebody else has more. The Yellow Woman tells me that everyone is trying to use me and rip me off. The Blue Woman scolds me for not having a more well-developed social conscience. Though my personal instincts are to nurture the artistic side that comes naturally, these other women are always prodding. "You are too emotional, too impractical, too impulsive." As much as I love my granny boots and peasant skirts, I think, *Perhaps I should go for a more corporate look, I mean, if I ever expect to be "management material."* The end result is a closet bulging with costumes.

My tug-of-war with these women is evidenced by the chaos of my physical surroundings. My bathroom looks like a testing laboratory for shampoos, the plastic bottles lined up like torpedoes along the rim of the tub. Similarly, my makeup table is a jumble of day creams, night creams, eye shadows for daytime looks and nighttime looks, and lipsticks that are all the wrong shade. Next to my bed, the nightstand is piled high with half-read self-help books. I'm afraid to put them away, lest I forget completely my obligation to know why I love too much, am compelled to control and can't seem to access my inner child. With all this clutter of confused identities, I sometimes wish halfheartedly for a fire to burn the place up—as if the refining flames would burn away all that's false and pasted on, to reveal the self that God created me to be, shining like a new penny among the ashes.

It's sad, isn't it? To be all grown up and not have a clue who we are—yet convinced that whoever we are must be defective Who of us don't have a whole chorus of voices in our heads—parents, old boyfriends, siblings, teachers, kids on the playground—tormenting us with orders to shape up, conform and otherwise get ourselves fixed? We spend outrageous sums of money on diet programs, therapists and health-club memberships, believing that there are in fact perfect people out there—we know, because we've seen them—and if we keep working at it, we'll be perfect someday too. Sooner or later, if we keep shooshing along on that NordicTrack, we are bound to arrive on the Planet of the Mauve Women.

In truth, I think that under all these layers of color, there is a Paisley Woman just dying to get out. You know the Paisley Woman, don't you? She's the one who snorts when she laughs. She might have a few chin hairs she has to tweeze each morning. And no matter how much she exercises, she can't lose those saddlebag thighs. Yet, in spite of all these "flaws," she likes herself. She knows she probably won't win any beauty contests, but it doesn't matter, because she knows it's not looking good that counts. She learned a long time ago not to base her self-worth on the Mauve Woman standard. She understands there is only one Person who warrants that kind of awe. And that Person doesn't layer his fragrances, coordinate his bathroom accessories or drive a Lexus.

I was encouraged the other day when I spotted the Mauve Woman in the airport. She was marching purposefully toward her departure gate wearing a pair of spectator pumps. Her Gucci bag glided behind her on a leash. The aggressively floral scent of Giorgio wafted in her wake. She had just one minor problem: static cling.

As we both ascended the escalator to our concourse, she tugged helplessly at the back of her silk dress. The more she tugged, the more it clung. By the time we reached the top of the escalator, that thing looked like it was plastered to her backside with superglue. Finally, she veered off toward the ladies' room.

So, even *they* can't maintain the façade for long! Sooner or later, a nail will break, the Nina pumps will get scuffed, coffee will spill down the front of that Vera scarf. It's one of the lesser-known laws of the universe. And those of us who haven't a single pair of runless pantyhose can count ourselves vindicated. What a relief!

Your beauty should not come from outward adornment, such as braided hair and the wearing of gold jewelry and fine clothes. Instead, it should be that of your inner self, the unfading beauty of a gentle and quiet spirit, which is of great worth in God's sight. (1 Pet 3:3-4)

9

Adrift in the Sargasso Sea

Day after day, day after day,
We stuck, nor breath nor motion;
As idle as a painted ship
Upon a painted ocean.
—SAMUEL TAYLOR COLERIDGE

In the middle of the Atlantic Ocean there exists a body
of water called the Sargasso Sea. Distinctly separate from the
ocean that surrounds it, it can be distinguished by the beds of
seaweed that sway beneath its relatively still surface and the
unique sea life adapted to its special ecosystem. Romantic poets
of two centuries ago spun lurid tales of sailing ships becalmed
in the Sargasso Sea, where their sails hung lifeless from their
masts and crews slowly died from thirst and madness.

Sometimes, in the inexorable ebb and flow of life, there will be moments when you feel adrift in an in-between place that feels suspiciously like the Sargasso Sea. Days cycle by with a numbing sameness. It feels as though you are running on automatic pilot from the moment you fumble for the buzzing alarm clock to the boring commute to your predictable job to your nightly appointment with *Wheel of Fortune* to that last lethargic striptease as you fall into bed to start the cycle all over again.

For me, it's that psychic purgatory where the pleasant memories that sustain me through fallow times grow faint and the future looms like a nebulous shadow. Nothing in my environment speaks of nurture. I can't remember the last time someone put their arms around me, and I feel something deep within starting to wither from neglect.

When you are single and perhaps prone to be isolated with your problems, it may be doubly hard to make headway against the tide of monotony that threatens to drown your dreams and swallow your hope. You may not have the kind of friend who will come alongside and coach you through extended black moods. I'm reminded of that scene in the movie *Moonstruck* where Cher slaps a despondent Nicolas Cage and orders him, "Snap out of it!" It would be nice to have some handsome celebrity around who could serve that purpose (for me, Sean Connery will do nicely, thank you). But when you are single, it is more likely you will be left to slap yourself back to reality.

Now, to some degree, I think there is purpose to spells of "soul drift." Those moments when we are becalmed in a Sargasso Sea provide the perfect opportunity for uninterrupted communion with the Creator and a chance to restore him to his rightful place on our list of priorities. But having said that, when your boat is going nowhere, sometimes you have to stick your paddle in the water and row—even when there are no stars to navigate by and no land in sight. Sometimes you have to muster movement when the muse is silent, motivation is nil and your extremities feel like potted plants.

I may invite howls of protest from some in the counseling field who would insist this idea promotes "dysfunctional" thinking, but I think there is a grain of truth in the saying "Act happy and you'll be happy." There is something about physical movement that stimulates the brain as well as the circulatory system. Pretending you have a reason to get up in the morning may trigger something deep in the stagnant backwater where your mind used to be—something primordial and foreign—egads! A *creative thought!* As you go through the motions of taking a night class in conversational Japanese, you might experience a fleeting but pleasant sensation called *interest.* As you force yourself to make friendly conversation during a Bible study, you may be surprised by a strange sound erupting from the depths of your diaphragm—*laughter!*

Yes, sometimes it requires something as basic as putting one foot in front of the other. Doing a lot of stuff you may not feel like doing. Why? Because when you are depressed, *nothing* sounds appealing—except maybe another pint of Ben & Jerry's double chocolate chunk ice cream and a long nap.

And another thing. When you are searching for purpose in life, nothing stirs a sense of purposefulness better than making yourself available to others. There is a world out there of hurting, lonely people. Those who say, "I am no good to anyone else until I get myself fixed," are not only copping out on their responsibility to their fellow human beings but dooming themselves to social isolation. All of us are damaged in some way. We walk around with patched-up places, parts missing, stuffing hanging out. If we hole up somewhere waiting for emotional healing to take place before we are willing to step out into the world, we deny God the opportunity to use us—brokenness and all—to bring about tremendous blessings in others' lives.

So don't think in your wasted emotional condition that you have nothing to offer. If you have a hand, you can hold a hand. If you have a strong back, you can help deliver food to the local soup kitchen. If you have a car, you can drive a senior citizen to the grocery store and back. As mechanical as these acts may seem, at some point the hand will start to connect with the emotions. The connection may be faint at first, like nerve endings reattached after surgery to a traumatized limb, but the transference will happen. And when it does, it will be like breathing a lungful of fresh air after what seemed an eternity under water.

As a veteran of countless therapy groups and as someone who has wrestled with serious bouts of emotional and spiritual ennui, I can tell you there is no way out but through. It helps to be keenly aware of destructive patterns in your life and to be willing to seek counsel if necessary. But if you are like me, you recognize the cyclical nature of things. God will not leave you forever to flounder in the Sargasso Sea. He will send a cleansing tide. You will again experience the exhilaration of the ocean spray on your face, the fullness of billowing sails and a sense of starting fresh on a new adventure.

In the meantime, take the advice of an old song: "Row, row, row your boat . . ."

Cast your bread upon the waters,
   for after many days you will find it again. (Eccles 11:1)

10

It's Only a Movie

If I have one resolution this year, it is to *not* watch *When Harry Met Sally.* You know the story. It features a ridiculously attractive couple who go through an entire movie arguing the premise that men and women can't be friends—then the guy has an epiphany and proposes to the girl in the middle of a dance floor on New Year's Eve. Though hip and contemporary in tone, *When Harry Met Sally* perpetuates a Cinderella fantasy that renders my nonfiction existence about as fascinating as stale bread. Likewise *Pretty Woman* and *Sleepless in Seattle.*

Don't get me wrong. I love a good romance as much as anyone. But when I am having trouble reconciling the images on the screen with my life down here in nontechnicolor reality, the messages these movies convey only reinforce false beliefs about love and relationships—and about what I conclude everyone else must have that I don't.

There is a place in our lives for fairy tales. Unleavened by occasional flights of fancy, the daily grind would make for a drab existence indeed. The danger comes when we allow our perceptions of reality to be shaped by fairy tales. And the people who create popular songs, advertising, TV shows and movies are experts at infiltrating the subconscious with messages both subliminal and overt about what is attractive, desirable and normal.

To most movie makers, reality is a big-haired, cellulite-free Julia Roberts, Mel Gibson's impossibly handsome profile, show homes overlooking picturesque bodies of water, and fascinating high-paying jobs with liberal lunch hours to facilitate witty dialogue over meals at trendy restaurants. In these movies, conversation is never peppered with mundane comments about bills or dental appointments. These people don't do laundry or watch game shows. They don't gain weight. And they never acknowledge the influence of God in their lives— they utter his name only as an expletive.

When I've been allowing movie fantasy to spill over into my perception of reality, it's interesting to note how low my threshold of tolerance is for men who are not classically handsome or who display less than heroic behavior.

In *Love Is a Feeling to Be Learned* (InterVarsity Press, 1971), Walter Trobisch tells the story of Sylvia and her prince not-so-charming. It's much closer to real life than most movies are.

* * *

It caused Sylvia almost physical pain to give up her dream. But now she was sure: This was the end of it.

Before she had met him, she had had a dream image of

what her future husband would be like: tall, slim, a good athlete, intelligent, full of spirit, a university graduate, a few years older than she, and, of course, a lover of music and poetry, possibly a professor of English literature or religion or a holder of a well-paid job with the government.

When she passed a florist shop and saw the dark-red roses in the window, Sylvia pictured to herself just how it would be some day when someone would bring her such roses as a declaration of his love.

Gone was the dream! He was so different. There was absolutely nothing exciting about him. When he had asked her for their first date she had prayed in her heart: "Please, Lord, not him! He's not the one I want to marry!"

She had never been interested in technical things and that was his whole field of interest, because he was a construction engineer. He also was rather dull. No, he didn't bring her roses. He didn't bring her anything. He just came and there he was.

He was so down to earth and so sober.

Not that he was without feeling. But just the expression of his feelings irritated her. She couldn't rely upon them, because they could change so quickly. One minute he was impetuous and enthusiastic and the next he was as solemn as a stick. When she longed for a tender word, he offered her a kiss instead, and in the same breath talked about football or his studies.

Everything was reason and will with him. He called her stupid and sentimental when she put more faith in her intuition than in his reasoning and thinking.

Why can't a boy be like a girl?

Sometimes she wanted to be like a porcupine, roll together and show her prickles in order to make him understand in a thorny way that moonlight did not increase her desire for contact.

In his presence, she felt the desire to withdraw into the fortress of freedom and hoist the flag of independence.

Yet Sylvia did not send him away. Not yet, she thought; maybe later on.

But later on, a half a year or so, a few things dawned on her. She began to understand that a young man who sends a book to her which interests him, may be more serious than someone who sends roses.

The book says: I want to share something with you which moves my heart at present. I want to give you a part in my life. I want to know what you think. It is important to me to know what you think.

She discovered to her astonishment one day, that she had stopped to look at a bridge. For the first time she saw the beauty of its swing, of its lines. Or she stood and watched as the beams for a skyscraper were hoisted upwards and thought: I should show this to him.

It was no longer important to her just to be understood. She herself had begun to understand. She had learned the first lesson in love: one has to give up dreams, because they stand in the way of happiness.

Love is a special way of feeling—something to be learned.

* * *

Sylvia's dream, based on fairy-tale values, had to go. That lovely, soft-focus dream could have kept her from opening herself to something unglamorous but wonderful—something that perhaps ended up (though we don't get told the end of the story) bringing her forty or fifty years of happiness.

Sylvia learned what's really important about a man. She finally looked beyond the externals to see the person inside. That's what we women always want men to do; here's our chance to do the same.

So, when the lights go down in the theater and Mel's or Kevin's or Harrison's baby-blue eyes gaze down into yours from a forty-foot screen, you would be well advised to pinch your leg every few minutes and repeat the following words to yourself: *It's only a movie.*

When they arrived, Samuel saw Eliab and thought, "Surely the LORD's anointed stands here before the LORD."

But the LORD said to Samuel, "Do not consider his appearance or his height, for I have rejected him. The LORD does not look at the things man looks at. Man looks at the outward appearance, but the LORD looks at the heart." (1 Sam 16:6-7)

11

Attack of the Forty-Foot Invisible Woman

It's that time of the month when all that I yearn for, every dream that I aspire to, can be summed up in two words: pork rinds. It's PMS time! Food cravings run to the kind of things you see profiled in fuzzily filmed exposés on *Prime Time Live*. Ding-Dongs, Ho-Hos and other hyphenated foods become my sustenance of choice—with taste buds so corrupted by hormone fluctuations that they only register two sensations: salt and chocolate. And those two food groups are consumed in such embarrassing quantities as to require extreme security measures to ensure private, uninterrupted eating pleasure.

When PMS strikes, my perceptions become as distorted as reflections in a funhouse mirror. Crying jags erupt unexpectedly, triggered by sentimental Kodak commercials. I trip on invisible curbs and slam into doorways. Glasses fly out of my hand as though controlled by poltergeists. During this time, I am particularly vulnerable to feelings of invisibleness.

With antennae fully extended, my rejection detectors operate on frequencies normally reserved for spy satellites. They zero in on perceived slights from friends, employers, coworkers and miscellaneous rude restaurant personnel. They notice the merest critical flicker of an eyebrow; they magnify "Roberta, I wonder whether George's idea might work better" into "Boy, was your suggestion ever *dumb*, Roberta, and by the way, I never did like you." The resulting internal monologue tends to drown out saner voices, ricocheting off the inside of my skull like an errant mortar round.

Fortunately, most of my mental harangues don't make it past the guarded ramparts of pursed lips. But now and then a cagey, miscreant little putdown escapes. It masquerades as legitimate self-defense. It hides its barbs behind a veil of sarcasm or vague references to past wrongs. It disguises itself so cleverly that the person wounded by it is left mysteriously impotent to respond. Ultimately, it wreaks havoc on the relationship it targets, undermining trust and putting its victim permanently on guard.

PMS is a particularly frightful malady, one that I am relieved to see go into remission each month. But it does not give me the right to hurt others. If my attitude toward some person or circumstance is marked by resentment and bitterness, then I had better search for solutions to the problem and not use PMS as a handy excuse. PMS *is* real—just one more aspect of this wacky, wonderful world called womanhood. But I might be able to mitigate its symptoms if I learn to recognize and deal honestly with the nonimaginary emotions this cursed affliction only magnifies.

Fortunately, we have a Father who understands our PMS symptoms. And the fact that our crying jags and feelings of rejection are hormonally induced doesn't lessen his love for us or make our tears any less worthy of a gentle hand to wipe them away. To God, all our pain is legitimate. And where people may not always be sensitive to our feelings, he always knows. He always sees. We are *not* invisible. No matter how wretched, sallow-eyed, cranky and bloated we may feel, he loves us unfailingly and without condition. I think there's more than a little consolation in that, don't you?

Now, please pass the pork rinds and Midol—I feel another crying jag coming on. Don't you just adore being a girl?

Have mercy on me, O God, have mercy on me,
    for in you my soul takes refuge.
I will take refuge in the shadow of your wings
    until the disaster has passed. (Ps 57:1)

12
A Lone Ranger

June 1968. Our family piled into our mint-green 1963 Buick Electra with a cooler full of bologna-and-butter sandwiches and headed south for the Great American Vacation.

Our family vacations always began with everyone in high spirits. My sisters and I sang camp songs, dressed our Betsy McCall paper dolls and played road-trip alphabet to pass the time. Every hundred miles or so we pulled off the highway to stretch our legs at Stuckey's and hound our parents for rubber tomahawks and pecan logs—mind you, these were the days before golden arches ruled the interstate.

Of course, as the miles wore on, the initial giddiness dissipated. Soon weary of word games, my sisters and I elbowed each other and whined incessantly. Occasionally the back seat erupted with disgusted exclamations of "EEEEYEEW!!" as the car swerved around a sloppy heap of mangled roadkill punctuating an otherwise featureless highway. Meanwhile, Mom, the primary driver, gripped and regripped the steering wheel, her foot dancing agitatedly on the accelerator. Oblivious to the sensibilities of everyone else in the car, Dad puffed on a cigar and spit loose shreds of tobacco off the tip of his tongue. As the car filled with blue smoke and Mom continued her little jig on the gas pedal, the three of us in the back munched saltines in a vain attempt to ward off carsickness. So went Rand family vacations. I have been pursuing the elusive concept of stress-free, endorphin-producing holidays ever since.

Childhood road trips not withstanding, I love to travel. For a long time it seemed as if the ideal was to have companions to share vacation experiences with. Someone with whom I could point to the Eiffel Tower or the Grand Canyon or the World's Largest Prairie Dog and revel in the ecstatic communion of ooohs and ahhhs. We are conditioned to travel in herds—or at the very least, in pairs.

A while ago I decided to rethink my own reluctance to travel alone. It took a travel nightmare to open my eyes to the advantages.

A teacher friend and I decided to go to Europe together. Though Sharon and I were not bosom buddies, we shared a mutual enthusiasm for exploring a new continent. We spent the weeks prior to our departure purchasing the requisite backpacking equipment and planning our route. I dreamed of *Sound of Music* country—Austria. Her "must see" was Paris. We had three weeks to ride the rails.

What we didn't calculate were our very different philosophies of travel. While I was open to serendipitous changes,

Sharon felt more comfortable adhering to a set itinerary. Early in our train journey, we met up with some folks on their way to an obscure church in France. The church was rumored to have dazzling stained-glass windows that, when struck by sunlight at a certain time of day, cast fantastic mosaics of color in the church's Gothic interior. It sounded like a marvelous thing to see. Nevertheless, Sharon nixed the idea, and we stuck to the prearranged schedule—a document which, I soon learned, was to be treated with a reverence approaching religious zeal.

From day one, our journey was marred by a constant low-grade tension and the knowledge that we were stuck with each other for the next twenty-one days. And the idea of parting company and meeting up somewhere down the line was unthinkable. No, we were joined at the hip for the duration—even if it meant we would kill each other by the time three weeks were up.

Toward the end of our journey, on our way north toward Paris, we stopped for an overnight in Florence. I was totally captivated by this city that virtually breathed art. I begged Sharon to consider an extra day there, but by that time she was weary of traveling and was missing her boyfriend back home. For her, everything up to that point had been just a preliminary to the main event—Paris. So she gave thumbs down to any thought of spending more than one night in Florence. On the train the next morning, as I watched the Renaissance domes and spires of Florence recede into the distance, I secretly cursed the day I had agreed to this travel fiasco. I would hazard a guess that as Sharon dragged me, brooding, through the streets of Paris, the feeling was entirely mutual.

We were too young to recognize that such an undertaking—even under the guise of a "holiday"—can test the endurance of the hardiest of relationships. The combination of altered sleep habits and unfamiliar cultures can magnify petty differences, transforming them into major sources of strife. If you look closely, the pastoral landscapes of foreign countries are littered with the bleached bones of abandoned friendships—wrecked over arguments about where to eat and which castle to visit. Although Sharon and I couldn't have anticipated every single conflict that would arise on our trip, we might at least have been more prepared if we had sat down together and talked some things over beforehand. Here is a checklist of issues to discuss with your potential travelmate before you purchase those expensive plane tickets.

☐ Do you agree on accommodations? Perhaps one of you puts a premium on comfort—you will spend whatever it costs to get a full night's sleep. In addition, you consider a stay in a foreign hotel a way to soak up ambience. But your traveling companion frets over finances. She couldn't care less about ambience. She won't have peace of mind as long as she sees her shrinking American dollars gobbled up by expensive hotels. She'd much rather cut corners by staying in youth hostels—better yet, catch a few winks en route to the next destination. Be warned. Worried, sleep-deprived people are usually time bombs waiting to go off.

☐ If you savor the experience of dining in nice restaurants, while your partner prefers eating fast food on the run, you're going to have problems. Likewise if you are an adventurous eater who welcomes the opportunity to eat fried squid while the first thing your friend checks out in every major city is the exact location of McDonald's. Attitudes about food and shelter are basic. If you can't agree on at least those two things, you might want to think twice about risking the friendship!

☐ What's your philosophy of travel? Are you someone who likes to go with the flow, open to changes of direction—cool if things don't go quite according to plan? Or are you a "point A to point B" traveler who wants to know precisely where you are, exactly where you are headed and what time you are getting there? If you and your friend operate in different philosophical spheres where travel is concerned, chances are you will be a universe apart by the time you come home. "Star Wars" may be a more apt description.

☐ Does the person you plan to travel with have the same physical stamina you do? If your friend is overweight and out of shape, it's unrealistic to expect her to keep up with your vigorous stride during a hike up Pike's Peak—or even a marathon museum tour. If you do decide you want to undertake a hike together, set a pace that is comfortable for both. That might mean going at a slower pace with frequent rest stops. During my days in the military, when we did "company" runs, we always allowed the most short-legged soldier to set the pace for the entire group. You don't build team morale—or friendship—by leaving someone in the dust. If you insist that you want to cover ground quickly, make that understood at the very beginning. And weigh your priorities. Which is more important—keeping a friend or getting someplace fast?

☐ Even compatible people need a little solitude now and then. Before you board the airplane, discuss the possibility of scheduling time apart during your trip. Taking a breather from togetherness will alleviate stress and allow you both to indulge in your special pastimes and interests. Your companion may welcome the chance to lounge around the hotel swimming pool for an afternoon. While she does that, you can get some shopping done or explore a few of the historic landmarks you've been dying to see. Communication is the key. And remember: it isn't natural to be attached at the hip twenty-four hours a day for a week or more. Give each other room!

☐ Finally, what does this trip represent to you? A chance to see the world and your life from a new perspective? An opportunity to throw yourself body and soul into a new culture? Or are you basically someone who just wants to work on your tan, pick up a few souvenirs, snap a couple of pictures, and get home to your familiar surroundings?

During my own travels, I have noticed two particular types of travelers. One sits at an outdoor café on the piazza, sips a latte and tries to immerse herself in the sights, smells and sensations of a rare new experience. The other just wants to gather evidence. She keeps a video camera perched on her shoulder at all times, so that everything she sees is framed by a lens. Her objective is to cover the most territory in the least amount of time so she'll have proof of where she's been when she gets back home.

They are polar opposites, yet how many times do we observe this mismatched pair gamely trying to make a go of their so-called vacation and secretly wishing the other would just sort of accidently fall off the top of the Eiffel Tower?

Conditioned as we are to travel in pairs, we tend to view lone travelers as exotic misfits or people to be pitied—surely they must be lonely. And the specter of being lonely in a foreign culture is so unpleasant that we conclude even being shackled to someone we hate is a more desirable fate. But in truth, the fear of traveling alone limits us. It inhibits spontaneity. And it keeps us from experiencing new, potentially rewarding friendships. People who travel in groups or even with just one other person tend to discourage casual approaches from strangers. That may be a preference for travelers here in the States, where we are all cowed by the threat of crime. But in some parts of Europe, where mass transit is the preferred mode of transportation and people are still relatively safe, it is not unusual for strangers to strike up conversations with each other.

What is the potential for such casual meetings? When I was stationed with the Army in Augsburg, I took frequent trips to Munich, a forty-five-minute train ride away. One afternoon, on the return trip, I entered a second-class compartment and sat down across from a girl in her mid-twenties. She had long, unruly hair and a pretty face with an impossibly warm smile. Having pegged me as an American (we Yanks can't seem to fool anyone), she introduced herself as Sylvia.

I tried my best to utilize my fractured German, but after exhausting my elementary vocabulary ("Ich liebe Deutschland!"), I finally surrendered and let her carry the conversation in her much more fluent English. By the end of our short train trip, we had struck up a friendship and exchanged phone numbers.

Over the next two years, Sylvia and her boyfriend Axel plied me with chocolate and cappuccino, introduced me to their friends and family and showed me sights in Bavaria that tourists seldom see. Sylvia and I also shared an interest in folk music. Many evenings were spent strumming old John Denver songs, accompanied by Axel on the bongos. After I left the Army and returned to the States, we kept in touch.

Axel and Sylvia married a few years ago and now have two

darling little girls, whom I got to know on my last trip. I have been back twice to see them—the last time they were so anxious for a visit that they paid for my flight! Over the years, Sylvia and I have become close friends—her term is "sympatico." We send each other birthday cards, and every Christmas we exchange care packages. All of this is the result of a chance meeting on a train.

As for my prematurely shortened stay in Florence, I vowed that I would return someday and stay as long as I wanted, doing whatever I wanted while I was there. Five years after my first visit, I went back—alone. I set up my base of operations in a tiny room at a charming *pension* not far off the Ponte Vecchio. For a week, I methodically explored churches, museums, markets and piazzas—and never once felt lonely. Occasionally I hooked up with other hotel guests for a meal or a stroll in the evening, and then retired to my room, culturally sated. That week in Florence was the best vacation I ever had.

I would be remiss if I did not admit to solitary journeys where the bugaboo of loneliness did rear its ugly head. One particular trip to Greece had some very lonely moments. Like the gray day I rented a motor scooter to explore Santorini's northern tip—an uphill journey all the way. The scooter malfunctioned and I pushed it for two miles in the rain before a sympathetic pair of honeymooners threw the bucket of bolts in the back of their Jeep and carried me back to my hotel.

Or the day I convinced some fishermen anchored just off the beach to let me come out to their boat to mingle for a while (if my mother had only known the chances I took!). The boat's captain could have been the model for Zorba the Greek, as he guzzled retsina and danced around the deck before passing out in his cabin. After a meal of fishhead soup washed down with

ouzo, I grew ⌐
crewmen had to
deathly sick for th⌐
anything for a sympath⌐
over the toilet.

I also confess that suns⌐
preferably shared with *someon⌐*
male gender. Nevertheless, it is
foolish to miss simply because I m⌐
set of eyes.

God's creation is varied and vast. We s⌐ ⌐n every
opportunity to view his handiwork. Remer⌐ ⌐t wherever
we roam on the planet—no matter how dist⌐⌐t from all that
is familiar and comfortable—he is our constant companion,
and he always speaks the language. When you think about it,
who better to share the ecstatic communion of oohs and
ahhhs with than the Artist himself?

The "double-occupancy blues" are a predictable part of
solo travel, but they are fleeting. And if it's any consolation to
you, I have found that they produce some of my best journal
entries. So cast off your fears and hit the road. Remember me
when you stop at Stuckey's. I even give you permission to buy
a rubber tomahawk.

Blessed are those who have learned to acclaim you,
    who walk in the light of your presence, O LORD. (Ps 89:15)

I Ha
Holio

buried longings and pro...
I end up feeling a...
my apartment...
Playing the Tuba at M...
on...

Christmas! Bah! Humbug!—EBENEZER SCROOGE

It's September. I'm still safe. I'll be okay for October
too. At least for most of it. But come the last two weeks of that
month, when the leaves begin to spiral off the trees in a final
poignant ballet before winter, I'll draw the remnants of Indian
summer around me like flimsy armor and brace myself for the
barrage of "family" holidays—Thanksgiving and Christmas—
followed by the couples' holiday, New Year's Eve, and finally
that day that disguises itself as a benign confection but feels,
at least for this single woman, more like marzipan-coated
barbed wire: Valentine's Day.

I admit it. I hate the holidays. The focus on families stirs

...okes discontent with my single state. ...bit like Charlie Brown, staring forlornly at ...nt-sized Christmas tree and wishing I could just lie ...beach in Mexico until the season passes. Consequently, the phrase "I hate the holidays" has evolved into almost an incantation to ensure maximum misery for me and anyone within hearing distance.

One thing that hangs me up year after year is my idealized vision of what holidays are *supposed* to be like. I don't know where these expectations come from; holidays of my youth were not the stuff of Norman Rockwell paintings. When I was growing up, the Christmas season was marked by financial and emotional stress, sleepless visits to the homes of distant relatives, car trouble, dreary weather and extreme hyperactivity triggered by overdoses of simple carbohydrates. Those carefully composed photos taken for the family Christmas card almost always held clues to the bickering that had gone on before the shutter clicked—red-rimmed eyes, braids askew, and one pudgy little face determinedly cross-eyed (guess who?) to foil the best efforts of any photographer.

I think the media can be blamed for much of it. Commercials advertising everything from coffee to greeting cards reinforce the illusion that somewhere out there is a misty, sepia-toned world where affluent, nondysfunctional families gather around designer Christmas trees in tableaus of undisrupted harmony. No wonder, as the saying goes, reality bites.

There is no such thing as the Christmas (or New Year's or Valentine's Day) of my fantasies, and until I release my insistence that such fantasies come true for me, I will never get a handle on the cloud of depression that descends in mid-October and doesn't lift until spring.

I am tired of being cowed by the calendar. I don't like having to shut down emotionally for four months out of the year. I have spent decades mourning dateless Valentine's Days and solitary Thanksgivings. It's time to shed my widow's weeds and reshape my expectations of holidays. Perhaps plan some new traditions. Instead of curling up in the fetal position on the couch for the entire month of December and blubbering through multiple airings of *It's a Wonderful Life,* I could designate the Christmas season as a time to practice those "random acts of kindness" I have been postponing all year. On Valentine's Day, I could invite my single friends for a dinner party complete with candlelight and Michael Bolton on the stereo. It may not compare to having a real date, but at least we can commiserate over our arid love lives and perhaps even find a reason to laugh.

Contrary to what many singles think, we are *not* the only ones who spend holidays holding loneliness at bay. There is no shortage of human beings who spend most of their days alone with only the talking heads on their TV sets to keep them company. The question for me has become, do I want to go on being part of the problem or would I rather look for ways to be part of the solution? I may not be able to alter my circumstances, but I can adjust my attitude.

It may sound hackneyed to recommend acts of kindness as a way to combat loneliness and feelings of worthlessness. And I don't suggest that visiting a nursing home or volunteering at the local homeless shelter will banish holiday depression completely. But it is a step. There is something transforming about reaching out to someone for whom social isolation is a fact of life 365 days of the year, not just during the holidays. When you consider the times you have felt starved for a loving touch, imagine the gift you could give an old woman just by holding her hand in yours for five minutes. And then contemplate the gift she is giving you. An accumulation of such experiences may cast holidays in a perspective that makes them not just tolerable but, for the first time in your adult life, a heartfelt reason to rejoice.

A *new command I give you: Love one another. As I have loved you, so you must love one another. By this all men will know that you are my disciples, if you love one another. (Jn 13:34-35)*

14

The Godzilla of Loneliness

One of my ongoing battles is learning to deal constructively with loneliness. Just when I think I've got it licked, one of those long weekends sneaks up on me when no solitary activity can distract from the desire to be with other human beings. I'm like the guy in the Arby's commercial running down deserted streets screaming, "Where did everybody go?"

During those times I am most vulnerable to spending sprees and chocolate binges. Sitting glassy-eyed before the television with remote control in hand, I cycle through the channels—a junkie searching for a fix. Before long, I'm on a first-name basis with the hosts of all the home-shopping networks and my credit cards are maxed out with purchases of cubic zirconias and skin products made from sea slime.

For those of us who flee loneliness with the blind desperation of the citizens of Tokyo fleeing Godzilla's earthshaking
footfalls, it is an exhausting enterprise. In its looming shadow,
we escape to shopping malls, where we further medicate
ourselves with unnecessary purchases and attempt to simulate
the feeling of connectedness by merging with throngs of
fellow shoppers. We lurch from one activity to another, hardly
pausing to ponder the reckless expenditure of energy and
resources. We drive. We watch movies. We make long-distance
phone calls. We turn the stereo up loud—anything to hold
Godzilla at bay. But eventually, when the money is all spent
and the gas tank is empty, we must alight somewhere. To
confront the shrill voice in our heads. To do battle with the
Godzilla of loneliness.

In 1988 I met Tina. We were two of several government
investigators imported to St. Louis to conduct background
checks of people needing access to classified information. A
veteran in the field, Tina was my age, single and drop-dead
gorgeous. She had the clean, fresh beauty of a model in a
Noxzema ad. And she was smart. Eyes an intense Nordic blue
projected a laserlike intelligence. One got the impression that
Tina was always taking everything in, constantly storing information. She didn't seem especially fixated on her beauty, and
her whole demeanor discouraged others from being distracted by it. Tina was a professional, competent and business-
like. She would not be mistaken for a bimbo.

Even so, at the end of the workday, Tina easily shed her
tailored suits in favor of comfortable sweats. When all the
investigators—most of them ex-military men—congregated
in the hotel lobby to trade "war stories," Tina was there
holding court in her reserved, confident way, completely at

ease with these rumpled Columbo wannabes. I remember thinking at the time, *I wish I could be more like Tina. She's a woman completely comfortable in her own skin.*

Imagine the shock when, less than a year later, on a cold, drizzly day in March, my supervisor announced at an office meeting that Tina had been found dead in her Dallas apartment, shot in the heart—a victim of suicide. The note she left read, "I'm tired of being alone."

Sometimes it's a misty fog that lingers briefly and is easily dispatched with a good night's sleep or a welcome phone call. Other times it's Godzilla, crushing hopes like toy cars, shorting out all perspective—pop, pop, pop—like miniature telephone wires in its path. Ironically, the more elaborate our efforts to escape from loneliness, the bigger and more malevolent its shadow grows.

The Bible is filled with characters who experienced monumental bouts of loneliness—from Job, abandoned by his friends and feeling cut off from God, to Jesus in the Garden of Gethsemane, pleading with his disciples to stay awake just a little while to see him through the dark night before events accelerated to their necessary yet horrible conclusion. None described the experience of loneliness with more candor or eloquence than King David.

My heart is blighted and withered like grass;
  I forget to eat my food.
Because of my loud groaning
  I am reduced to skin and bones.
I am like a desert owl,
  like an owl among the ruins.
I lie awake; I have become
  like a bird alone on a roof.

All day long my enemies taunt me;
　　those who rail against me use my name as a curse.
For I eat ashes as my food
　　and mingle my drink with tears
because of your great wrath,
　　for you have taken me up and thrown me aside.
My days are like the evening shadow;
　　I wither away like grass. (Ps 102:4-11)

David, the consummate warrior, slayer of giants, knew that the scariest giants of all are not the flesh-and-bone variety but the vaporous, indwelling kind that haunt the recesses of our minds and defy us to come at them with our measly slingshots. He knew that the only way to do battle with a faceless foe is to meet it where it lives, using the weapon of faith and a willingness to experience pain to disarm and subdue it. In the same way he had confronted Goliath as a young man, David planted his feet and measured the distance—but this time the battleground was as close as his own tormented soul. Stripping off his armor, he exposed his heart to the enemy's insults. In yielding to difficult emotions, David emerged victorious over them again and again.

It seems so simple. If you only had a companion, you would never be lonely. But it's one of the ironies of loneliness that people are not necessarily the cure. Loneliness visits married people, attractive people, rich people and popular people. In fact, loneliness is one more symptom of our fallen human condition. One more reminder of our physical separation from the God we yearn for. Only in heaven will there be permanent relief.

One of the healthier activities I engage in when I feel lonely is to explore a wetlands area south of where I live in Colorado

Springs. There is something about being near water and the marsh wildlife and the smell of boggy earth that stills my soul like a tranquilizer. I can't help but draw comparisons of this experience to the familiar words of the Twenty-third Psalm.

What a consolation that the David who wrote of such bleak emotions in Psalm 102 also penned Psalm 23. From his words perhaps we can draw the courage to stop running from Godzilla's shadow, turning instead to embrace him and watch in wonder as he is transformed into a lamb.

The LORD is my shepherd, I shall not be in want.
He makes me lie down in green pastures,
he leads me beside quiet waters,
he restores my soul. (Ps 23:1-3)

15

Mr. Right

It was February. The tail end of a gray, lonely weekend. Escaping the confines of my apartment, I jumped in my truck and headed south. Fifteen minutes later, I pulled up to the elegant façade of the Broadmoor Hotel. Scurrying self-consciously past uniformed doormen, I made my way through the marbled foyer and onto a terrace overlooking a small lake. Strolling couples walked arm in arm. I sighed at the sight of their fading reflections in the water. As I dreamily tossed bread crumbs to the ducks, I sensed a familiar presence.

"Hello, Roberta." Out of my subconscious materialized a perfectly sculpted vision of masculinity—muscles bulging beneath his tweed jacket, a book of Yeats poetry tucked under one arm. His facial features were indistinct except for dark eyes, heavily lashed, gazing intensely into mine. It was Mr. Right.

"I thought you'd never get here," I sighed, savoring the sweet smells of tobacco and suede. The ducks didn't seem to notice.

"I love you," he whispered in accented English. "Will you marry me?"

I opened my mouth to say yes—then the sun disappeared behind the mountains and he was gone.

Years ago, I lay exhausted on a beach in Greece, painfully aware of the honeymooners frolicking in the surf. After a week on solitary holiday, scrambling over ancient ruins, exploring the narrow alleys of whitewashed villages and taking in breathtaking vistas of turquoise water, I suddenly felt weary—the cheerful single soldier was suffering from battle fatigue. I couldn't lie to myself. I longed for a companion. Behind my sunglasses, tears began to flow, sliding down my cheeks into my ears. Then there he was. Mr. Right. Whispering endearments into my ear—in Italian.

His mythical image is stoked by years of longing for a Protector, a Companion, a Lover, an Intellectual Equal, a Soul Mate—and Someone to Take Away the Pain. Mr. Right knows intuitively how to be all these things. Strong, yet sensitive. Loving unconditionally. Anticipating every need. Perceptive of every unexpressed emotion. Intercepting all the unpleasantries of life.

It would be the perfect relationship . . . if only he existed in real life. But, of course, he doesn't. He can't.

Because a man can't take away all the pain. Nor can he protect you and me from all the sharp edges in life. A man in your life doesn't guarantee you won't get lonely or have to change a flat tire or deal with mean-spirited people. Because no matter what your fantasies tell you, a man is still just a man.

Please understand. Women need men. Men make life interesting and exciting. Nothing makes a woman feel more womanly than a man's admiring gaze. And men's physical strength and grasp of abstract concepts are a perfect complement to our more intuitive, nurturing natures. But there is a difference between the mature desire for male companionship and inflated, unhealthy delusions about what such relationships can do for us. Too often our desire for love resembles something perilously close to idol worship.

So, whenever I find myself indulging in daydreams about Mr. Right, it's a good idea to counter those daydreams with a reality check. Just what triggers these fantasies? Fatigue? Stress at work? Have I recently run a gauntlet of wedding showers? Have I grown too socially isolated?

If you and I have fallen into bad habits, then we need to correct them. Arrange our lives so we get the rest our bodies need. Avoid those activities that leave us feeling emotionally depleted. Seek fellowship with same-sex friends and others with whom we can safely share our feelings of anger or sadness. We may not entirely banish unhealthy fantasies from our minds, but we can at least take a measure of control over our thought lives. And we should remind ourselves that relationships happen not in the six inches of gray matter taking up the space between our ears but in the world of sharp edges and rude sales clerks.

Yes, it can be a dangerous place, but it's the world we inhabit. And, as a matter of fact, we do not face it alone. There is Someone to turn to.

Find rest, O my soul, in God alone;
  my hope comes from him.
He alone is my rock and my salvation;
  he is my fortress, I will not be shaken.
My salvation and my honor depend on God;
  he is my mighty rock, my refuge.
Trust in him at all times, O people;
  pour out your hearts to him,
    for God is our refuge. (Ps 62:5-8)

16
Getting a Life

Years ago, before she finally got married, Chris called to say she was buying a house. She had even put down a $300 deposit. In spite of what seemed like happy news, she was subdued. Later she called me back to say she had changed her mind—and forfeited her $300. When I asked why, she explained that she was afraid that buying a house was like an admission she was never going to get married: house = spinsterhood.

It's the voodoo theory of romance. Cross a certain line and you jinx your chances for ever finding a mate.

Too many of us singles live in a perpetual state of suspended animation—with one foot planted somewhere in the vicinity of our senior year in college and the other dangling in the twilight zone of anticipation of our real lives, i.e., marriage. Until real life starts, everything is temporary—life is lived in increments, just in case. We don't own; we rent. We eat all our meals from a box. Our kitchen appliances consist of a toaster with only one slot that works and an electric mixer that throws off sparks on the low setting (not that we would actually cook something that required such high-tech preparation).

As graduates of the particle-board-and-cement-block school of decorating, we don't own anything that can't be disassembled easily for bi-yearly moves. Our furniture is vintage Goodwill. We've considered investing in a sofa, maybe a new mattress to replace the one we inherited from Grandma. But we don't do it, because these are the decisions we always thought we would make with our significant other. We aren't ready to surrender—not yet. Maybe if we just hang on a little longer, we won't have to admit to the cold, hard possibility that there may not *be* a significant other. Forget about a hope chest. The symbol of our existence is a cardboard box.

We labor under so many illusions—illusions that we control fate just by the thoughts we entertain and the things we wish for. Contrary to one brand of confused logic, there is no rule stating we aren't allowed to create a comfortable nest for ourselves. There is no sign on the door at Ethan Allen that says "Married People Only." Nor is it written that a single woman can't buy a house or set a pretty table. Stylish living and singleness are not mutually exclusive. Stop putting your life on hold out of some nebulous fear that it's not ladylike to take charge of your own happiness.

Now, it's essential that we keep a healthy perspective on temporal things and not resort to using "stuff" to fill the spiritual and emotional voids in our lives. Our sense of contentment and affirmation should come from God, not from possessions, position or status. But neither is it healthy to engage in superstitious thinking about what married women deserve that we don't. Equally damaging are faulty belief systems—if we jump through the right hoops, maybe deny ourselves certain things, God will ultimately give us the elusive desire that our years of self-denial have transformed into an idol. It's a game that can leave a woman resentful and bitter. And it will have her exchanging a present bursting with possibilities for a future that never arrives.

When we do begin to let go of "future" thinking, there is bound to be a period of grieving for those stubborn dreams that haven't come true. It should also be noted that shifting our focus doesn't mean those dreams may not yet happen. It simply means that we have allowed God to take over the reins. Freed up to grab on to the promises of the present, we might just be pleasantly surprised by the blessings he has been saving up for us.

Finally, it isn't enough to just count those blessings—as good stewards of God's gifts, we should be constantly on the lookout for opportunities to share them with others. Being single, we are uniquely positioned to minister to people in a lot of nontraditional life situations. If we are blessed with a house, we can make the space available for Bible studies and other church events. A spare bedroom can double as a temporary refuge for a woman in a crisis pregnancy. A large dining room table can host a lot of "strays" around Thanksgiving and Christmas. By creating an environment that invites strangers to become friends, we also go a long way toward fulfilling our own emotional needs.

No, we may not have control over whether we marry or not.

But we needn't sentence ourselves to lives of denial and desperation, either. There is validity—and yes, satisfaction—in being single. So rifle that hope chest. It has stayed locked up long enough.

> *A gift opens the way for the giver*
>   *and ushers him into the presence of the great. (Prov 18:16)*

> *Each one should use whatever gift he has received to serve others, faithfully administering God's grace in its various forms. (1 Pet 4:10)*

17
A Word About Men

Few things pierce the heart more than loving someone who doesn't love you back. Unreciprocated love and the hunger for intimacy are probably the biggest challenges there are to a woman's pledge to live gracefully single. I wince when I think of the times I have sacrificed my dignity, my common sense and my Christian values in the pursuit of someone who had no interest in pursuing a romantic relationship.

When you have feelings for someone, you think there must be *some* way you can make him want you. Maybe if you lose weight. Or if he sees how intelligent and witty you are. Perhaps if you cook him a great meal. Or if he sees how popular you are with people who count. And when nothing else works— and you have the self-image of compressed dirt—perhaps, you reason, he'll want you for sure when he finds out what a good lover you are. Sex used as a trump card.

Ironically, the man will probably leave anyway—but not before he has taken you up on your free offer. It's endemic in the secular world, but sadly, Christian men and women are also guilty of engaging in these games of sexual barter.

In a PBS series called *Getting Love Right,* psychologist Terence Gorski makes the point that many of us are attracted to people who are not emotionally equipped to meet our needs. He tells the story of the man who finds a frozen snake in the snow. He brings the snake inside, lays it on a pillow by the fire, feeds it hot soup and nurses it until it thaws out.

Finally, the man reaches out to pet the snake, and it bites him. The man draws his hand away in shock and implores the snake, "How could you bite me after all I've done for you?"

The snake replies, "What did you expect? I'm a snake."

If I took a poll, a lot of folks reading this would likely admit to a history of falling for snakes. We jump through all kinds of hoops in an effort to attract men who may as well be deaf, dumb and blind.

Even in the throes of the realization that we have wasted our energy on a hopeless cause, we will continue to beat a dead horse. Not long ago, I developed a crush on a man at work. We engaged in a brief correspondence in which we exchanged minor secrets about ourselves. In one of his letters he indicated that one of things he desired most is a woman who is kind. I assured him that I was indeed kind. He appeared to be amenable to pursuing the relationship, but nothing further happened. After not hearing a word or receiving any phone calls, I decided to make my move. I sent him an invitation to a party with an RSVP request. He didn't reply.

Frustrated by his lack of response, I began to fume. Annoyance at his perceived lack of courtesy eventually escalated into full-blown rage, vented to my counselor.

"Why are you so angry?" she prodded.

"Because it's rude not to reply to an RSVP."

"But why would that make you so angry?"

"Because he says he wants a woman who is kind, but he's not behaving kindly himself."

"But what is it that's at the root of your anger?"

"I want him to want me, @#%!"*

And that was the bottom line. I couldn't make him want me. Fortunately in that case, the relationship fizzled before it began, sparing me a prolonged bout of shameless maneuvering for his nonexistent affection.

But that hasn't always been the case.

There was a time in my past when the longing for love clouded my thinking, blotting out every vestige of good judgment. I didn't have a bulwark of concerned friends, a well-developed sense of self-worth and the spiritual maturity to avoid the pit of sexual sin. And I call it sin, because terms like "self-destructive impulses" tell only part of the story. In any case, the experience left the shrapnel of reckless liaisons embedded in my psyche and lopped-off pieces of my self-esteem littering the beds of indifferent men. It has been a long, slow journey back from the abyss. If you've been there, you know of what I speak. If you haven't, it is not a place you want to go.

Women: Believe me when I tell you no man is worth compromising your body, your soul or, most of all, your relationship with Christ for. The damage you do to yourself—and to others—in the process can have devastating implications for the rest of your life.

When the longing for love drives you to your knees, use that posture to its full advantage by presenting your longing as a sacrifice to the only One who experiences your pain as his own. No, he may not send you roses and chocolates. He offers only the promise of his profound and inextinguishable passion.

I have chosen you and have not rejected you.
So do not fear, for I am with you;
   do not be dismayed, for I am your God.
I will strengthen you and help you;
   I will uphold you with my righteous right hand.(Is 41:9-10)

18

Broken Statues

My home is furnished with antiques. I love combing flea markets and yard sales for vintage bed linens, scraps of velvet and odd pieces of old china to add to the general ambience of faded gentility in my small apartment. I have always labored under the assumption that old things are better than new. And perhaps underlying that assumption is a nostalgia for a sense of permanence in a world where nothing lasts—not appliances, jobs, marriages, values or people. There is something comforting about heavy old furniture that was never meant to be moved from one room to another, let alone to an opposite coast.

But lately I'm reevaluating this philosophy. I'm beginning to process the idea that old is not necessarily better.

When I first moved to Colorado Springs eight years ago, I lugged along with me a large record collection. At that time, music stores still stocked LPs. CDs were only beginning to nudge their way into the bins. Those little rainbow-colored disks didn't seem a technological threat at the time. So assured I was that vinyl would remain the preferred format for recorded music for generations to come that I even bought a state-of-the-art turntable with a walnut base and expensive needle and cartridge. But within two years, CDs exploded onto the market, spelling doom for the space-gobbling, scratch-prone record albums I had always loved.

At first, I lived in denial of the new technology. Visits to Goodwill yielded a harvest of records at bargain prices as I stocked up on classic albums by Pure Prairie League and the Doobie Brothers. The problem was that I never seemed to get around to cueing up the stereo and putting the platters on the turntable.

Now I am anticipating a possible move. The vertebrae in my lower back are already compressing in protest at the prospect of lugging all those records, stereo components and speakers from one place to another. My treasured collector's items are looking more and more like dead weight as I contemplate the obvious: dinosaurs became extinct for a reason.

Antique stores usually have shelves full of cast-iron food grinders—the ones with a long handle that Grandma once used to grind up everything from apples to sausage. Though they qualify as "collectible," most people much prefer their Cuisinarts to these bulky, hard-to-store monstrosities. I inherited one. Stumped as to how to display it, I finally clamped it to the window sill with a dried-flower arrangement in its maw. My attempt to utilize this appliance in a way so contrary to its original function seemed froufrou and undignified. So now it once more takes up precious space beneath the kitchen sink, keeping company with the Drano and the Brillo pads.

What to do with gadgets that qualify as "antique" but have been rendered obsolete by time, technology and changing needs? Our reverence for artifacts prevents us from tossing them out. Relics like padded tea cozies, steamer trunks and 12′ x 6′ linen tablecloths with faded cranberry stains are condemned to the purgatory between consignment shop and landfill.

During my tour of duty in Germany, I took advantage of the many inexpensive tours of the region. One of those tours took me to Lake Chiemsee in Bavaria. In the middle of that big lake is an island with one of several castles commissioned by the infamous "mad" King Ludwig. Ludwig based the grandiose Herrenchiemsee on the blueprint for the Versailles palace in France. As with most of Ludwig's castles, Herrenchiemsee is a kitschy, ostentatious version of the edifice it was meant to imitate. The grounds around it feature formal gardens, fantastic fountains and the ubiquitous statues of nude nymphs, seraphs, gods and goddesses.

During my day on the grounds, I explored the fountains and gardens and snapped pictures until my film ran out. Then I put the camera away and began poking around some of the secluded, less visited areas adjacent to the castle. Following a service road that veered off into the woods, I stumbled upon a spooky, surreal sight. There in the shadows cast by low-hanging trees was a huge cage filled with the twisted limbs and oxidized torsos of broken statues. Was it the insult of war, or perhaps the less dramatic but equally decimating effect of acid rain, that had transformed winged cherubs and Teutonic warriors into just so much scrap metal?

Gazing upon the pitiful remnants of a bygone century— those streaked, dismembered bodies unabashedly commingling in full view of an American tourist—I felt like an intruder. As though the inexorable process of decomposition was meant to transpire away from my prying eyes. And I felt sad. Not so much over the demise of a few arguably minor objets d'art or even the frailty of men's shrines to themselves. But all those rigid bodies crammed into that wire cage reminded me of the way we human beings get ourselves stuck. We tend to cling to people and things and places we outgrew long ago. We ignore opportunities, postpone choices and reject clear signals that a change is called for. Eventually we forget how to grow, and we become like broken statues—rigid, lifeless and pathetic to look at. Entrenched in our stale rituals, we have nothing to look forward to but a long, boring wait as time and the elements finish us off.

It's fine to treasure keepsakes, but we should be careful that our love for mementos doesn't mutate into mausoleum-sized obsessions with the past. Speaking for myself, I have to be careful that in my appreciation of old things I don't *become* an old thing. The memories of the music of my youth are a dozen times sweeter than the scratched-up carcasses of a bunch of old LPs. The detritus of ancient experiences only weighs me down and prevents me from taking hold of the next adventure.

So if you happen to see a forty-year-old woman whistling "Taps" as she hauls her record collection to the dump one day, don't be alarmed. It's only me making room for the new. By the way, I have this wonderful antique food grinder. A real collector's item. I can make you a deal.

Forget the former things;
*   do not dwell on the past.*
See, I am doing a new thing!
*   Now it springs up; do you not perceive it? (Is 43:18)*

19

Letting Yourself Go

F-F-Forty. I can barely get my mouth around the number. Lately, I look in the mirror and see tiny lines around my eyes, as telltale as growth rings on a tree. The stray gray hairs that for a while I could pluck and forget now defy pruning as they sprout in bunches around my temples. The first hint of jowliness tugs at my jawline. External body parts are shifting southward. Gravity is taking its toll.

Until now you may have postponed the physical signs of aging through diet, exercise and, if you are Cher, plastic surgery. But against your will and your best efforts, your once supple flesh is beginning to show the elasticity of a Spandex swimsuit run through the dryer on the sturdy/permanent press cycle. All stretched out and no place to go. Your looks are fading. The only thing to do is say goodby to any hope of a love life and twiddle your thumbs for the next half-century or so—*not!*

Few things bring out the rabid feminist in me more than the idea that when a woman's youthful appearance starts to go, so do her chances for romance or any semblance of a vital life. Where is it written that after she turns forty, a woman should cut her hair, don sensible shoes and resign herself to the role of onlooker in the pageant of life? Pardon me, but it is a "rule" which I choose not to observe.

It may be that a lot of men don't recognize the truth in the sentiment expressed by Augustus McCrae in *Lonesome Dove:* "The older the fiddle, the sweeter the music," but I mustn't allow the prejudices of unenlightened men to affect my belief in my own unique beauty—which may include gray hair, crow's feet and sagging thighs. For me, one of the benefits of age is that I no longer have to be enslaved to an unattainable, media-imposed definition of beauty. I can rest—at last—in the knowledge that my "imperfect" body is okay with me and with the One who created it. I can go on a diet if I want to—even cover the gray if it lifts my spirits. But I do it for *me,* confident that I am still beautiful, no matter what my age or body configuration. And if some insensitive male ever dares to accuse me of "letting myself go," I can reply in all confidence, "Yes, I have let myself go—to make room in my life for self-acceptance and to occupy my thoughts with more substantial things than craving your approval."

So, girls, let's stop treating ourselves as though we were tacky paintings on black velvet. With the layered hues of life experience to provide depth and dimension, we are master-pieces who only grow more valuable with age.

For you created my inmost being;
   you knit me together in my mother's womb.
I praise you because I am fearfully and wonderfully made;
   your works are wonderful,
   I know that full well. (Ps 139:13-14)

20
Security

In 1961, my parents, my two sisters and I moved from the tiny house we had outgrown into a house my mother called her dream house—39 Marshall Place. Located in a comfortable middle-class neighborhood bordered by woods and adjacent to rambling "old money" estates, Marshall Place was a bucolic oasis on the fringes of the city of St. Louis. The two-story, turn-of-the-century houses nestled on large lots with deep, gently sloping lawns and majestic two-hundred-year-old trees whose limbs intertwined high in the air to form a green canopy over the entire length of the street. We girls spent long afternoons in their sun-dappled shade, casting our Barbie dolls in dramas that alternated perilous escapes with frequent costume changes.

Marshall Place teemed with children. There were elaborate birthday parties and swarms of us catching fireflies at night and playing hide-and-seek in the endless woods. My friend Mimi and I imagined that we were the wild ponies of Chincoteague as we whinnied and galloped the length of our back yards. On sticky August days, we retired to the shade of a stand of pine trees where we napped on beds of fallen pine bows.

To this seven-year-old, Marshall Place was a place of safety where no demons dared to intrude and children roamed unencumbered by grownup concepts of time or fear. At day's end, I would fall into a deep sleep in the middle of my big bed, fully confident that, when morning came, the adventure of childhood would resume without interruption—as it was surely bound to do tomorrow and the next day and the day after that. It seemed a perfect place. And when we had to move away, there were many tears, because we all thought we would live there forever. It never occurred to us that danger might be lurking in the enchanted woods where we had acted out fairy tales untainted by the threat of villains. But there was a villain. We didn't learn about him until many years later. The pimply teenager followed the unselfconscious movements of six- and seven-year-olds like a hungry hyena sizing up a herd of gazelles. He was able to carry out his particular brand of evil with total impunity, for a cunning abuser knows a child's shame is enough to seal her silence long after he has moved on to his next victim.

What other cruelties must have occurred behind the façades of those grand old houses? Faint rumors of abuse and violence circulated among the grownups, but the cultural taboos of the time ensured that they remained neatly hidden away. "The heart is deceitful above all things and beyond cure. Who can understand it?" (Jer 17:9). There is no end to the creativity people apply to their evil acts. And no one is above suspicion. Not even children.

A few years ago, I became obsessed with buying a house. At a difficult time when the whole world seemed to be shifting under my feet, I viewed that accomplishment as my key to peace of mind. I drove endlessly up and down the streets of Colorado Springs, scribbling down information from "For Sale" signs. Sometimes at night I'd walk the old downtown neighborhoods, savoring the aroma of steaks cooking on back-yard grills, relishing the green smells and hissing sounds of lawn sprinklers and the laughter of invisible children playing in those back yards. The lights glowing from within those warm sanctuaries conjured up memories of Marshall Place—my standard by which security was measured.

But there is no security in a house, any more than there is true security in a marriage or the love of a parent or a hefty IRA. No, security comes from only one place. And the dimensions of that place are exactly the dimensions of the room you make in your heart for Jesus Christ. Remember that the next time you feel jittery about the immediate future or begin to fear a lonely old age as a bag lady. Look inside your heart for a warm room with a hearth where the fire never goes out, the love is real and permanent, and neither thieves nor the enemies of children can break in and steal it away.

I will lie down and sleep in peace,
for you alone, O LORD,
make me dwell in safety. (Ps 4:8)

My people will live in peaceful dwelling places,
   in secure homes,
   in undisturbed places of rest. (Is 32:18)

Jesus replied, "If anyone loves me, he will obey my teaching. My Father will love him, and we will come to him and make our home with him." (Jn 14:23)

21

Lost in Space

It's an unthinkable thought . . . but it hovers there, triggered into awareness as I watch my mother cross her arms tightly across her chest and purse her lips in what looks suspiciously like a pout. She never used to do that. Or when my writer father laments in a sloppily typed postcard that he's losing his memory. He checked the bank deposit box for a silver pocket watch. It wasn't there. Did he give it to me? Or to one of my sisters? You gave it to me, Dad.

It wasn't so long ago that My Mother the Dynamo perched fearlessly on a ladder under the eaves, paintbrush in hand, casually waving away the wasps. She's still pretty fearless, but she moves more tentatively now, balancing gingerly on feet and ankles swollen with arthritis from repeated sprains.

My father has a sensual nature, a love of beauty and a journalist's zealous curiosity about the world. His need to engage all of his senses and to seize the fleeting moment has at times been a source of exasperation to those close to him. On family outings years ago, it wasn't unusual for him to bring the car to a stop on a bridge over some woodland creek. There he would bolt from the driver's seat, strip down to his shorts and dive into the water while the rest of us groaned in embarrassment. Now, his once ruddy cheeks sag beneath eyes red from insomnia. He still enjoys the beauty around him, but he doesn't dive into swimming holes anymore.

My parents are aging. In a few years, they will be gone, and I'll be "out there" on my own in a new way. The small town that I spent years trying to escape but still refer to as "home" will be just another burg off the interstate, the record of my time there only as permanent as a childhood playmate's memory. How do I adjust as my identity as child of my parents shifts to that of parent to my parents, and finally—orphan? Without a husband and children of my own to cushion the transition, who will be my touchstone? Where will "home" be?

Recently, during a vacation with my mom, I began to fully absorb the implications of the changes taking place in her appearance and behavior. For the first time, I glimpsed a future without her. On one especially harrowing night, I lay awake vibrating with fear, straining to hear her breathing in the bed next to mine. *Please don't let her die, God. Please don't let her die. Not yet.* Then something happened. The sense of desolation and paralyzing panic ebbed away, replaced by an almost insular calm. In an instant, the invisible hand of God had reached down and shooed away the demons, replacing them with his transcendent peace.

I have been one of the lucky ones. Until now, death has taken only those whose lives marginally intersected with mine. With only a few exceptions, the dark adventure of grief has mercifully brushed by me. But my life will not remain charmed forever. One day in the not-so-distant future, I will experience grief's icy hold upon my heart. When that day arrives, I pray that my emotional ducks will be in a row—with pains from the past fully reconciled and no unfinished family business to complicate the grieving process.

Until then, my confidence rests on the only One who can promise that he will never leave or forsake me. No, he doesn't offer me the assurance that my mother will always be here, but, in my foretaste of grief, he has shown me that he will provide the exact measure of strength I need to endure my grief and a promise of rest in the midst of mourning. I am so thankful for this God whose tears mingle with my own and who reminds me that I am not lost in space but protected, listened to, loved. With him as both Mommy and Daddy, I will never be an orphan.

For I am convinced that neither death nor life, neither angels nor demons, neither the present nor the future, nor any powers, neither height nor depth, nor anything else in all creation, will be able to separate us from the love of God that is in Christ Jesus our Lord. (Rom 8:38-39)

22

Permission to Hope

In our sleep, pain that cannot forget falls drop by drop upon the heart and in our own despair, against our will, comes wisdom through the awful grace of God.

—AESCHYLUS

So many men, so few brains." "They found something that does the work of five men—one woman!" "Women are generally smarter than men." "God is coming back—and boy is she p@##d." These are bumper stickers I saw recently on a parked car outside my counselor's office. I didn't know what had transpired in the owner's life to trigger her need to turn her car into a moving billboard that in essence screamed at the world, "I hate men!" I could imagine, though.

It seems so easy for men. While they lie prone in their La-Z-Boys and read nothing more introspective than the sports page, we take aerobics classes and devour self-help books. As we angst over cellulite and search for swimsuits that both are stylish *and* have the figure-contouring properties of whalebone, they saunter unselfconsciously around crowded beaches with pasty bellies spilling over their Speedos. Even more galling is the sight of men our age basking in the attention of giggling twenty-year-olds, the furrows and gray hair only enhancing their desirability—a metamorphosis that only spells the extinction of romantic possibilities for us. Men unabashedly pass gas. We hold it in. And hold it in. And hold it in. Is it any wonder that some of us snap?

And yet, I can't help feeling sorry for the woman with the bumper stickers. She has surrendered to bitterness. Where she once hoped to love and be loved, she now desires only to wound. If it was legal, she would probably like to plow her cute little bumper-stickered Honda into a crowded sports bar.

Instilled in us from childhood was the message, both spoken and implied, that someday we'd get married and raise families of our own. No other options were presented. And though a few fearless individuals overcame their conditioning to take roads less traveled, most of us continued to wait patiently, heads down, eyes glued to the appointed script, repeating over and over again the words of Mark 11:24: "Whatever you ask for in prayer, believe that you have received it, and it will be yours." After years of nursing that hope and fervently believing the promises our mothers made, how were we to process the alien information that maybe marriage wasn't in our futures after all?

For me, it meant a long spell of avoiding weddings and baby showers and secretly resenting the happiness of newly engaged women. I detested men—and women for wanting them. Inevitably, my anger at the human race led to an indictment of God. I quit going to church because it seemed God was taunting me with pews filled with couples and families. I could easily have been that woman with the bumper stickers. The destructive downward spiral finally led me into counseling.

Eventually I was forced to take inventory of my priorities and to correct some wrong assumptions about God. One of those assumptions is that because I *want* something desperately, it is a *need*—and a *right*. I may protest to God that I don't have the "gift" of singleness, but ultimately God determines my needs. If my earthly longings override my desire for a right relationship with God, I won't be satisfied with what he gives. Then I can't help but be outside his will. And that will inevitably lead to disappointment—even in the Holy Grail of marriage.

My prayer for you and for me is that we will learn to desire God above all things. And perhaps when the hunger for that relationship transcends everything else, sweeping new vistas will open up for us—vistas that render our dreams of matrimony, along with our other unmet needs, no more than tiny specks on a horizon of limitless possibilities.

The flip side of this truth is that God gives us permission to hope. The reason we hope is not that we will necessarily receive all that we hope for, but that a life devoid of hope does not qualify as life.

My old friend Chris called recently, and somehow we got on the subject of weddings. "Chris," I protested, "we really shouldn't talk about that subject. It causes me pain." Wisely she said, "Whether you talk about it or not, you're in pain. Let's plan a wedding."

And so we did. We planned my dress, the music, the cake, the flowers and the guest list. It didn't matter that there wasn't a groom. It was just fun to indulge in the hope. In the middle of the "arrangements" I could hear Chris's baby crying. It was time to bring our conversation to a close. After hanging up the phone, I was surprised that the old familiar ache over things related to marriage was no longer there. My once swollen and unmanageable yearning had somehow, almost imperceptibly, shrunk down to the size and significance of any other lifestyle choice.

With marriage deposited alongside all my other hopes, I can now take comfort in knowing that should a particular hope never be realized, there are many more to take its place. Having abundant stores of hope to fuel my life's journey, I can fly high and free—a solo flight, to be sure, but oh what a ride!

And we rejoice in the hope of the glory of God. Not only so, but we also rejoice in our sufferings, because we know that suffering produces perseverance; perseverance, character; and character, hope. And hope does not disappoint us, because God has poured out his love into our hearts by the Holy Spirit, whom he has given us. (Rom 5:2-5)

23

Coloring Outside
the Lines

I have decided to trade my Tupperware dreams for a different kind of adventure. I will no longer view my singleness as a condition to escape from, limping through life wearing the expression of a deer frozen in oncoming headlights as I ponder a partnerless future.

It is time to jettison the psychic baggage that has kept me nearsighted and hidebound for so long. From this day forward, I will celebrate my identity as an uncommon woman and actively pursue a "designer" life—one that makes the most of my particular gifts and circumstances. I will follow where my dreams lead, listening for God's direction, accepting his verdicts with grace and trusting that he has my best interests in mind, even when my limited perceptions tell me differently.

In setting my sights on a particular goal, I will keep in mind that the world is overflowing with naysayers—people who make it their special mission in life to dissuade me from taking risks and who love to relate stories about other people's shipwrecked dreams. As I weigh my choices in life, I will steer clear of naysayers and instead search out the counsel of one or two wise cheerleaders—people of discernment who will tell me hard truths but who also believe in my abilities.

Though I won't be afraid to "dream large," I will temper my visions with a healthy dose of realism. I will focus on goals that are not dependent on the whims of another person, lest I die a frustrated, bitter woman—with stiff, cold fingers that must be pried from a single dream that didn't come true.

I will do all I can to dispel the world's misconceptions about single people (we're irresponsible, arrested in our emotional development, single because there must be something wron with us). I will actively promote single women as leaders and role models in the church and workplace, alerting both men and women to the wealth of talent, creativity, intelligence and insight that single women have to offer—and I will attempt to accomplish these things with a minimum of male-bashing!

I will stay in circulation, meeting people, taking emotional risks, striving for authenticity in all my relationships. I will devote myself to the hard work of communication, taking inventory of my progress as I go along: Am I listening? Am I asking questions? Am I speaking a language that others can understand?

I will do my best to avoid a narrow, "singles only" social milieu, instead cultivating friendships with all kinds of people, married and single. By the same token, I will strive to be sensitive to the limitations of married friendships and not harbor resentment when their "couple" concerns take precedence over mine.

I understand that there will be lonely times. Times when I crave the physical touch of another human being. Times when I ache for a child of my own. Far from denying my desire for intimate relationships, I will be honest with God about those feelings. But I'll waste no more time ruminating on threadbare notions about how life was supposed to work out. And I will resist interpreting my singleness as a sign of God's punishment or his rejection or as evidence that I am undeserving of marriage. Whenever I find myself caving in to the mindset that singleness is a "second-class" lifestyle, I will keep one thing in mind—Jesus was also single.

I acknowledge that with no traditional family of my own to be a consistent source of strength and support, it is important to cultivate a broad base of friends and acquaintances—people to whom I can turn in times of crisis and who can confidently turn to me in their own times of need. I also resolve to accord friendships with women the same respect and importance as friendships with men—and stop treating my fellow females as social adversaries.

I will not be afraid to consider nontraditional solutions to questions about career, church, relationship-building, home and finances. As a single person untethered by marriage or parenting commitments, I have limitless options. As long as my decisions are based on healthy motives and harmonize with God's commandments, I can feel free to make those choices that enable me to be a happy, well-adjusted person. I have permission to do as the commercial says and "go for the gusto!"

Having put all these noble aspirations to paper, I allow that I will fail at all of them at one time or another. When it happens, I will cut myself a little slack, have a good cry if it's called for and vow to do better tomorrow.

There is a great little quote attributed to Queen Victoria. "It is good to be queen." Contrary to some interpretations, I don't believe this saying is about arrogance. I believe this perfect nugget of understatement conveys a much bigger message. It is this: When I am secure in who God made me, all the striving and posturing and insecurities will be a thing of the past. The compulsion to prove my worth to the world will be done with. After all, who questions the credentials of a queen? A queen need not react defensively against people or circumstances—everyone knows that only a slave finds it necessary to revolt. A queen knows she's loved and accepted—after all, she *is* queen, isn't she?

Perhaps the queen analogy is a stretch. But to restate it in less cryptic terms: It is good to know who you are. When you are secure in your identity as a treasured child of God and have finally decided to trust his intentions for you, you are freed to devote your energies to those pursuits that really count—mainly furthering the kingdom of God. Freed from the panic of having to control every circumstance in our lives, you and I *can* live gracefully single. And while we may struggle with our less queenly attributes, we can rest in the assurance that at the end of this search for understanding, a King is waiting.

And I—in righteousness I will see your face;
when I awake, I will be satisfied with seeing your likeness.
(Ps 17:15)